PRAISE FOR *SMART WORK U*

"Our nation is under a mountain of debt; this book helps the next generation avoid this problem from the start of their career. Real world tips from someone who has walked her talk. *Smart Work U* is the first textbook college students should buy."

— Jim Batten, Executive Vice-President, Convoy of Hope

"Hona Amer's determination and personal experience really motivate students to believe that they are able to achieve their goal of graduating from college. This book is a "must read" and includes excellent study habits I wish I would have known before entering college. It contains other tips that I will use as I currently complete my degree. *Smart Work U* also gives insight on how to balance other important aspects of life while in college; ranging from finances, to friendship, to self confidence, and finally to walking across the stage in your cap and gown. This book is a minor investment now that will potentially save you valuable time and thousands of dollars on your college journey!"

— Alex Garcia, college student, Missouri State University

"This book is a great overview of the college experience for any student. The knowledge that is packed into this book can help a person from any background as they begin their college journey. *Smart Work U* is a concise book that contains all the needed information to achieve your goals in college and even help you graduate early. Hona's wisdom and knowledge will help anyone achieve their goals and have a great college experience."

— Dr. Dustin Cox, Physical Therapist

"*Smart Work U* is brilliant! A well written, insightful, highly practical guide every college student should read before wasting unnecessary time and money. It's more than theory...Hona Amer applied these secrets to her own educational journey before she wrote about them in this great book. This plan really works!"

— Scotty Gibbons, National Youth Speaker, Author *Overflow, Carry-On,* and *First Things First*

SMART WORK U ℠

get your degree
the smart way-
save time & money

HONA AMER

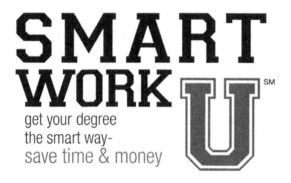

SMART WORK U
get your degree
the smart way-
save time & money

Published by Life Notes Press

ISBN: 978-0-9837166-0-0

Published in the United States of America.

DEDICATION

To my parents,

R.C. and Karen Amer,

who taught me the importance of perseverance, family,
integrity, and the value of education. Thank you for the legacy
you have passed on to me. I love you both.

To my sister,

Heather Chérie Amer,

who challenges me to continually grow while
being an example, encourager, cheerleader, and best friend.
Thank you for always believing in me.
Your friendship has changed my life for the better.

CONTENTS

CONTENTS CON'T

ACKNOWLEDGEMENTS

I would like to say a heartfelt thank you to the following people...

To my father, R.C., who always has ideas, suggestions, and support, while proofing the manuscript countless times. You continually challenge me to grow as a person, leader, and writer.

To my mother, Karen, who always encourages me through the ups and downs of life. Your consistent support, love, and encouragement propel me forward. When I wanted to stop writing, your words were wind in my sail.

To my sister, Heather, who read every page of my manuscript and countless articles yet still believes in me. I am grateful that you tell me the hard truth, when needed.

To Dawn Josephson, who reads manuscripts with a sharp eye and provides editorial expertise and insight. You helped make my dream a reality.

To Summer Morris, who designs with great attention to detail. Your work exceeded my expectations.

To my grandfather, Robert L. Thomas, who has always taken interest in my education, career, and life. Your words of wisdom have impacted my life.

To Mr. Bernie Dana, who is a trusted college advisor, professor, and mentor. You helped me succeed, even when I didn't fit the traditional mold of education.

To Dr. Alina Lehnert, who is a professor and role model of a young professional in the world of academia. I will never forget one significant conversation you had with me as I was choosing my college major. Your wisdom and insight were invaluable.

To Scotty Gibbons, who instilled in me a continual desire to know and love God. Your leadership, passion, and commitment are influencing a generation.

To Trevor Birch, the first person outside of my family to call me a writer. Your words have encouraged me countless times.

To my greatest inspiration and best friend, Jesus Christ—my source of hope, my Savior, and guide on this unique journey called life. May my life communicate Your Message.

To You, the reader, thank you for taking time to read this book. May my journey encourage you that anything is possible.

PREFACE

a s I stood in the midst of a sea of people—all gathered to celebrate a significant accomplishment—I felt frozen in time. Years of work collided into one day, one moment, one profound celebration.

I smiled.

This was not the kind of smile you give as a courtesy to people who make a joke and no one laughs. This was the kind of smile where your skin can't stretch any farther and it remains plastered on your face for hours...even days.

I was excited for a million reasons, but I smiled for one: I had graduated from college with my Bachelor's degree—and I did it in only two-and-a-half years.

The present moment would soon be a distant memory, but the accomplishment would last a lifetime.

College Graduation...a million reasons to smile.

INTRODUCTION

"I figured if you're going to do something,
you should do it the best you can."
– John T. Walton

I s it possible to go to college for two-and-a-half years and graduate with a Bachelor's degree? I did. You can, too. In this book, I am sharing the principles, techniques, and strategies I used so you can make your way through college and graduate in less than four years.

Here's the best part: You don't have to be a genius or a know-it-all to save time, money, and energy. With a little discipline, motivation, and a clearly defined goal, you will be well on your way to a college degree in less than four years.

GET OUT FAST

The modern college experience is very different than it was a generation ago. When my father went to college, his goal was to get a degree in order to prepare for a job or career. This was before the Internet, before the proliferation of home computers, and before the fast-pace digital world we live in today. Going to college for four or more years for a Bachelor's degree was just the way it was. There were no online course offerings, no research at your fingertips, and no technology tools to make disseminating information quicker and easier. The only way to speed up the process was to be a gifted academic prodigy.

These days, things are much different. We're a generation who grew up multi-tasking. We have technology that enables us to do things in a fraction of the time it took to do them just ten years ago. We text, we Skype, and we log onto everything, from banking to ordering a pizza. Yes, life is much different.

So shouldn't our college experience be different too? Since we get information in new ways, since we have to process so much more data, since we have new technology at our disposal, is going to college for four years to earn a Bachelor's degree really necessary?

I proved that it isn't.

Whether you're tired of school and never want to sit in a classroom again, an overachiever who wants to get out into the "real" world quickly, or simply someone who wants a faster college experience, this book will help you.

While I am a big proponent of being a lifelong learner, being a lifelong undergraduate student in college will accomplish nothing for you. College is a passageway that people go through to prepare them for life, as well as a career in a chosen field. The college years are a critical time for self-development, yet development should continue throughout all the stages of life. Therefore, there's no reason you have to sit through four long years of college classes to get the degree you need or want. You can get in, get out, and then get on with life.

HOW TO USE THIS BOOK

I wrote this book with a few assumptions in mind. Knowing them will help you make the most of this information.

- **Assumption #1:** You have already graduated from high school and are either entering college soon or have recently started your college journey. Don't get me wrong...if you're still in high school, you can definitely use this book as a valuable tool to help you plan your college experience. However, I wrote it with the perspective of someone in college now. So if something doesn't apply to you yet, rest assured that it will in the near future. Additionally, if you've been in college a bit longer than you'd like already, the information here will help you get on the fast track so you don't prolong your education any longer.

- **Assumption #2:** You are serious about college; you simply want to fast track your education. I know that some people go to college as an escape from the responsibilities of life and to prolong their adolescent years. If that's you, and you actually want to stay in college for as long as possible, that's fine. Just realize that this book is designed for someone eager to graduate sooner rather than later.

- **Assumption #3:** You're a regular college student, just like I was. While I always took my education seriously my entire life, I am by no means a genius. If you're one of the rare super gifted people who skipped grades throughout your life and graduated high school at age 12, you can probably teach all of us a thing or two. For the rest of us regular folks, this book will show you real, everyday strategies anyone can use to speed up your college experience.

FAST TRACK TIP

FAST TRACK TIPS will point out specific steps or action items that will shave time from your college years. Implement these as soon as possible.

And since I know you definitely don't want another long and boring textbook to read, I've made this book easy to navigate. As you go through this book, you'll notice specific sections designed to help you process the information presented.

By making this book as easy to understand and implement as possible, I hope you will feel empowered and motivated to take charge of your college education.

SMART TALK

SMART TALK sections will reinforce a concept you absolutely need to know about succeeding in college in simple, straightforward language so there's no confusion on what you need to do.

YOUR FUTURE AWAITS

If you have any lingering doubts of whether college is really for you, I'd like you to shift your perspective a bit. Look at college as a time of preparation. Even though you could get a job right now for $8, $10, or even $15 an hour, is that job really what you want to do for your whole life?

FAST TRACK TIP

Go to college while you're young.
You have fewer responsibilities and people depending on you.

Let's face it...there is no better time to go to college than right now, when you are young. You have fewer responsibilities and people depending on you. The more "stuff" you acquire in life, such as a house, cars, or children, the higher your monthly expenses will be. You won't be able to just start taking classes when you feel like it. When people are young, they often have a perception that life will get easier as they get older. I have not found that to be true, and neither have the numerous people in their 30s, 40s, and 50s with whom I have spoken. The older we get, the more packed our schedules become, and the busy demands of life require our attention. You have to take other people into consideration. If you are considering college, make a good decision. Decide to go. It will change the rest of your life.

The fact is that when people put off going to college for one or two years, they are less likely to go at all. I once heard someone say that she didn't want to go to college; she just wanted to follow her dream right then. Well guess what... she's still trying to get her dream off the ground. I can't help but think how much further ahead she would be today if she had gone to college so she could prepare for her dream.

Don't underestimate the time of preparation. Your life is similar to building a house. To have a solid house, you need a good foundation. College is a layer in the foundation of your life that will enable you to go farther, jump higher, and dream bigger. When you are making your decision, overcome the obstacles, and you will be amazed how the college experience will equip you for life. College is an investment in your future.

SMART TALK

You must start college envisioning yourself as graduating. **If you don't think you will ever graduate, you won't.** If you think you will graduate and can picture yourself walking across the stage in your cap and gown, you will. Either way, you'll be right.

When you begin college, graduation day seems a million miles away. Here's a little secret: You must start college envisioning yourself as graduating. No matter what stage you are in life, you need a specific goal to follow, and you need to pursue that goal until you achieve it. If you don't think you will ever graduate, you won't. If you think you will graduate and can picture yourself walking across the stage in your cap and gown, you will. Either way, you'll be right.

So here are the secrets for navigating through college, graduating early, and not breaking the bank or losing your mind in the process. Your new adventure awaits you. Are you ready? Let's get started...right now.

CHAPTER ONE
Welcome To College

The difference between school and life?
"In school, you're taught a lesson and then given a test. In life,
you're given a test that teaches you a lesson."
– Tom Bodett

m ost people dream of the day they will go to college. It represents opportunity, freedom, and a new experience.

The first time I stepped onto a college campus as a college student, I was completely overwhelmed. The idea of going to college had seemed so distant for my entire senior year of high school. But there I was...about to start my new life as a college student.

Everything was going great on that sunny June afternoon. I was walking on the college campus where I would go to school in a couple of months. I had graduated from high school in May; now I was doing early registration in June. The breeze of freedom was guiding me on my cloud of possibilities. It seemed as if nothing could cloud my day.

But even on sunny days, rain clouds can pop up unexpectedly. Skies were sunny until I met with my new advisor.

I didn't know what degree I wanted to pursue, so I was an undecided major. Although this is not the label of the rejects, it is the label of the indecisive person—of someone who takes more than four years to get a degree. Everyone else seemed to have specific dreams of where he or she wanted to go and what degree to pursue. But there was a small group of students, myself included, who hadn't made that life changing decision yet.

Of course, I was very excited. I was on a cloud. Picking classes and scheduling is just one step closer to college actually starting. It all started to feel so real.

SMART TALK

It is important to enter your first meeting with an advisor **prepared for the experience.**

My first advisor was a very gracious lady and the person assigned to all the "undecided" majors. Her main goal was to help us discover what we wanted to do by advising us to take a variety of classes in different areas. Sounds like a good plan... if you want to be in school forever. However, I wasn't interested in being in school forever, and I wasn't interested in taking unnecessary classes.

The only problem was that I couldn't tell my advisor what I was feeling. She had a PhD in something posted on the wall behind her. I was just a young 17-year-old trying to register for college. Since I was intimidated, I said nothing. I just sat there and agreed to her plan of putting me in the most random history, English, and literature classes. I knew I didn't need any of those classes, but I was frozen in my chair. I left the building and cried. My first encounter with college had been an utter disaster. The rain started pouring.

"I am never going to college," I said to my mom as soon as I had left.

My hopes and dreams were crushed. It wasn't my advisor's fault though. She had no idea I left upset. I never told her.

Fortunately, my mom was unconvinced by my irrational attitude. She believed in me despite my initial setbacks, and she wasn't going to let me give up that easily. I am so glad she didn't let me quit.

She convinced me to go right back up to the advisor's office that same day. You could have probably heard my feet dragging from a mile away. This time, however, I was better prepared and wasn't doing it alone.

If you don't know the answers, it is smart to find someone who does. I took someone who was a current student at the school, my sister. Well, I think she mostly "took" me with her. According to her, we were going back up to that advisor's office no matter what.

When you are entering into a new experience, it is important that you consult someone who has been there before— someone who has done what you want to do. Sometimes, this person only has to be one step in front of you.

We all need people to be there for us when we want to give up. You might not have someone in your life you can consult, so consider me as your mentor for the remainder of this book.

So, how did that second meeting go? You know those days when there is an afternoon shower and then the sun shines again? You guessed it. The sun started shining again. The rain cloud dissipated, and the second meeting with the advisor was a success.

My sister knew which classes I should take and my preferences, and she diplomatically communicated my position to my advisor. She acted like a pro. While I was sitting in my chair feeling very nervous, she was confidently working through the details. I left the second meeting with my schedule in my hand. I was ready for August.

My first semester, I took 13 hours. Most students take 15 to 17 hours. I was a full-time student, though. Little did I know that in two-and-a-half years, I would be finished with college. How is that possible when I started at such a slow pace? That's what we're going to cover next. Do the steps I outline in this book and you'll be well on your way to repeating my success.

FAST TRACK TIP

The first secret to succeeding in college and graduating early is to **think about the end before you get there.**

START STRONG

The first semester of college requires you to get your feet on the ground. Many students go to college the first semester to have fun. However, the way that you start college will affect how you finish it. If you get a 1.0 GPA the first semester, you will have a hard time curing your GPA problems when you are a senior.

FAST TRACK TIP

Get the scoop on your professors from current students. **Choose one whose teaching style matches your learning style.** You'll do much better and won't have to repeat a class.

Therefore, the first secret to succeeding in college and graduating early is to think about the end before you get there. Each semester counts, because they build upon each other. It's easier to maintain a 3.0 GPA than to create a 3.0 GPA from a 1.0 GPA. So start college with the end in mind. Don't blow the first two years partying and pulling all-nighters—that's a sure way to a long and seemingly never-ending college experience. I'd even go so far as to say that you'd be practically flushing your life down the drain. You might think that is harsh, but the price you will pay for poor decisions will cost you more than you realize. Remember, college is the training ground for your life. Take time to develop positive habits that will stick with you for the long haul.

If you are going to commit to going to college, commit to doing your best, which looks different for everyone. Don't succumb to measuring your success based on other people. Do your best, and the grades and timing will take care of themselves.

NEW BEGINNINGS – NEW DECISIONS

When you are deciding on classes, ask someone about the various professors who teach the classes. Why? Because if you take classes from professors you like and who have a teaching style that matches your learning style, you'll do much better and won't have to repeat a class.

Repeating a required class is one sure way to add time to your college years.

Students usually have a lot to say about professors, and they will tell you about the professors' teaching styles, number of tests, and overall opinion. When you have an option of professors, you will benefit from picking the best one for you.

As for me and my journey, it was finally August. The back-to-school signs were in all the stores, and folders, pens, and paper were in high demand. I couldn't believe it was finally here—my first day of college. My heart couldn't have beat any faster. The adrenaline was flowing, and I was embarking on a new chapter of my life. Everything was new—new friends, new teachers, new campus, new parking lot, and new cafeteria. It was hard to know whether to be excited, nervous, or afraid. I was a mix of all these emotions.

The first day came and went. I met new people, sat through new classes, and overcame awkward moments. There is just nothing like first days.

When you start college, you will have many first experiences. If you are planning on transferring from a community college to a university, you will have to deal with transferring credits for the first time. Whether you are choosing to attend one school or you are going to a community college and transferring to a university, you really need to be aware of the classes you are taking and what you are able to transfer.

Don't worry...people transfer from one school to another all the time. You certainly won't be the first person in history to ever do so. However, when you are transferring from a community college to a university or simply between schools, you have to take into consideration the classes that are transferrable. You don't want to backtrack in your education by having to retake classes or take classes your new school requires but your previous one did not. Hence, it is important to make decisions about schools at the beginning of your college education.

Many community colleges have a state school nearby where their credits transfer. If you are aware of the classes that transfer, you will be able to save yourself time and money. Community colleges tend to have a greater compatibility with state universities because of their original design. However, if you are transferring between universities, you could be losing some of the classes, which translates into loss of time and money. It could also extend your education unnecessarily for a semester or even one or two years. Therefore, you need to figure out your transfer plan (if any) beforehand.

Realize that transferring schools is not always negative. If you currently go to a school in Florida and you transfer to a school in North Carolina, it might be a good decision for you for a variety of reasons: future or current work opportunities, cost of tuition, friends, distance from family, etc. Academically, you would be most benefited if you transfer during your first two years.

Weigh the pros and cons of the decision of switching. If the benefits outweigh the disadvantages of transferring schools, you should move ahead with your decision. It actually may be a great decision for you, considering all aspects of your life. For example, you may get married during school, which would require you to move. Look at it as an opportunity for a new beginning at a new school.

ENJOY YOUR NEW LIFE

When you train for a marathon, you envision yourself crossing the finish line each step of the training process. After all, what is the point of running the race if you never plan to finish? In the same way, you need to start college with the end in mind. You can not graduate in less than four years unless you have a clearly defined "finish line" for college. You have already decided to go to college. Congratulations! Now, decide to finish. Because you're taking time to invest in yourself, your future will be full of opportunity!

SUMMARY:

- When you go to college, it's a good idea to have a mentor. Consider this book as a mentor in your college journey.

- Your GPA matters. Don't blow off your first semester in college. If you get a 1.0 GPA the first semester, you will have a hard time curing your GPA problems when you are a senior.

- College is a layer in the foundation of your life that will enable you to go farther, jump higher, and dream bigger.

MAKE IT PRACTICAL:

1. Be prepared for your first advisor meeting by finding out class requirements and looking at a class schedule.

2. Ask a current student of the school questions about scheduling classes.

3. Be open and honest with your advisor. They are there to help you!

4. Ask a current student of the school questions about scheduling classes.

5. Be open and ready for all the new experiences you are about to have. Enjoy this time of your life.

CHAPTER TWO
Making New Friends

*"Put your heart, mind, intellect and soul even to your
smallest acts. This is the secret of success."*
– Swami Sivananda

even though you're going to college to further your
education, no one can deny that college is a very social experience. So rest assured that no matter how alone you feel
on that first day, you will make friends. Friends can be very beneficial in the college process, as you need fun, encouragement,
and people around you. However, the type of friends you choose
will have a significant effect on your focus and use of time.

FAST TRACK TIP

The people who surround
you will influence your
motivation, decisions,
and overall success.
Therefore, **choose
your friends
wisely.**

An old saying tells us,
"Show me your friends, and
I'll show you your future."
It is so true. The people who
surround you will influence
your motivation, decisions,
and overall success. Therefore, choose your friends
wisely. Be intentional in the
new friendships you are developing.

If your closest friends think that a "D" is good enough, you need new friends. Even if this "slacker" has been your friend since kindergarten, his or her attitude will affect your ability to move forward and graduate early. Friends who are not helping you succeed at life aren't true friends. If you want to become a winner, you must surround yourself with winners. Surround yourself with people who are internally motivated and have a balanced life. Don't give in to people just because you want friends.

Your new friends might be in one of your classes or live in your dorm. Wherever you find them, choose to befriend people who have dreams, goals, and passion about life. Their motivation will help you develop personal dreams and goals, which will be important not only for your time in college, but also for your future. Remember, college is just a time of preparation. It is only the beginning of surrounding yourself with positive people who will influence you to be all that you can be.

MORE THAN FRIENDS

Dating is a big part of the college experience, and some people meet their spouse in college. This doesn't mean they get married while they're still in school, as many people are getting married in their mid to late twenties, but still, dating is a part of college life.

> **SMART TALK**
>
> **Relationships take time and energy.** So be careful of the amount of energy you are investing in a relationship compared to other things in your life.

When you want to date someone, use the same criteria as you do for friendships. "Good looks" should never be your only reason for dating someone. Remember, someday that person will be old and have wrinkles! Relationships take time and energy. So be careful of the amount of energy you are investing in a relationship compared to other things in your life.

SMART TALK

Be confident in who you are and make wise decisions in regards to relationships.

When I was in college, I knew a girl who dated a different guy every week. Her life was so full of drama—a roller coaster of emotions—that she had little time for anything else. Talk about being emotionally drained!

Also, getting involved sexually in relationships before you are married will start a pattern in your life. In addition to the health consequences of possibly contracting a sexually transmitted disease, being involved in this level of intimacy outside of marriage will leave you hurt, disappointed, and possibly a parent. Abstinence until marriage is the only way to avoid this. No, I'm not a prude. I simply believe that if someone truly loves you, he or she will respect you. Be confident in who you are and make wise decisions in regards to relationships.

If your relationship is dragging you down, let it go. Be willing to wait for someone with moral standards, ambition, and dreams. Whatever you do, don't try to change someone; you rarely will. True change takes years and an internal desire to make the change. One month of dating is not enough.

If you do not find Mr. or Ms. Right and marry someone before you graduate from college, relax. You are likely better off. Take the time to pursue your own goals and dreams. Travel the world, establish yourself professionally, and get to really know who you are and what you value in life. Being in a romantic relationship is not the ultimate goal of college. Although you might meet someone who seems like "the one and only" when you are 18, realize that you change a lot between the ages of 18 and 22. So instead of jumping on a relationship rollercoaster, be careful about whom you date. And if you happen to find that lucky person in college, count your blessings!

DEALING WITH ROOMIES

We all like our own space. If you have a sibling, whether older or younger, you know how annoying it can be when people invade your space. Hence, learning to live with a roommate can be a challenge.

SMART TALK

Don't be afraid to confront your roommate—just **don't do it in the heat of the moment.**

The best way to minimize conflict is for you and your roommate to have two separate lives. Yes, you can be friends with your roommate, but if your lives are too intertwined, there is bound to be conflict. Therefore, as tempting as it is, I would not recommend being roommates with your best friend.

If possible, it's best to at least know the person before you become roommates. Agree up front that you will give each other space, and set clear guidelines for cleaning, buying food, dorm room visitors, etc. If you are living in an apartment and rent is due a certain day, establish rent and utilities payment percentages and schedules in advance. Most important, when you have conflict, talk about it.

Dealing with conflict is a natural part of life. Confrontation, though, is not very popular. People would rather avoid the situation than confront it, deal with it, and move on. Don't be afraid to confront your roommate—just don't do it in the heat of the moment. Talk to him or her about the problem when you aren't mad about it. Realize, too, that the other person might not even know there is a problem. By having open communication, you can discuss problems as they arise instead of bottling them up and exploding later down the road.

People often change roommates because of clashes in personality. You've seen the scenarios: You like to be clean; he could care less. You like to go to bed early; she thinks sleep is for when you are dead. Or, it might be an issue of conflicting schedules that causes problems. In that case, you can part on agreeable terms.

If you live in the dorms, you can usually request roommates, but that doesn't guarantee you'll get your request granted. If you don't like your roommate, don't panic. Find a new roommate the next semester. If you live on campus and there are serious issues with your roommate, talk to your resident advisor. Exceptions can be made for extenuating circumstances.

If you live off campus and are looking for a roommate, you can ask a friend, or contact the school. Sometimes schools will try to help connect people who are looking for roommates. I recommend "interviewing" your potential roommate before you commit to living with the person. Make sure you are both on the same page about basic things, such as work ethic, goals (the other person should have some), and importance of education. You also want to find out about their friends, as these other people will most likely be hanging out at your apartment. Ask them about their family, schooling, groups they are involved in, and former roommates. This should give you a general idea about the person. Finally, talk about such things as paying rent and utilities, cleaning the apartment, cooking, etc. These will all become issues at some point if you don't talk about them up front.

GET INVOLVED

Now that you have made it to college, get involved! Participating in activities is a great way to meet like-minded people. After all, chances are that if you both have a certain interest, you'd make good friends.

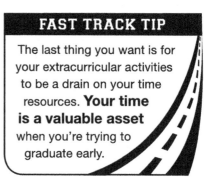

FAST TRACK TIP

The last thing you want is for your extracurricular activities to be a drain on your time resources. **Your time is a valuable asset** when you're trying to graduate early.

Colleges offer so many opportunities for students to get involved in activities, sports, or student government. Choose to participate in an activity that will be fun yet beneficial to your resume. You will often find that there are more activities to be involved in than you have time to commit. Therefore, when you begin college, pick only two or three extracurricular activities. Try them out and then choose one or two of them to pursue. The last thing you want is for your extracurricular activities to be a drain on your time resources. Your time is a valuable asset when you're trying to graduate early.

When I was in college, I decided that I was going to participate in the Activities Board, which planned social events for the school. It seemed like a fun thing to do based on my personality—I am a social person. I even knew some of the people on the board, so the interview went great! There were subcommittees within the Activities Board, and I was placed on the décor team.

Now let me paint the picture for you: By this time, I had chosen to be a business major (more on Choosing Your Major in chapter six). So here I was a business major with a bunch of artists and creative people. Our job was to create all different types of hand-made and painted stage décor, banners, etc. The artists and creative types loved doing this work; I, on the other hand, felt like poking my eyes out. Although it was fun to be around the people, it wasn't really a good fit. While they were all enjoying spending hours painting murals on foam board, I was counting down the minutes until I could leave. I stayed with AB the rest of the year but then decided it was time to move on.

Fortunately, the friendships I developed through being on the Activities Board lasted past my involvement. In the same way, the friendships you make in any activity can outlast your college experience. Since you are spending time with people outside of class, you have the chance to get to know them on a deeper level.

Some people find a niche and really enjoy it. If you can be involved in an activity you enjoy and that will benefit your resume, it is a double win. For example, a friend of mine was a journalism major, got involved with the school newspaper, and loved it. She would write stories, do layouts for the paper, and collaborate with the other team members. It gave her great experience and helped her land a journalism job after college.

BECOME A NETWORKER

While you should definitely associate with people in your area of interest, it's also good to get to know other people from different walks of life. Through interacting with your peers, you are learning to relate to a variety of people. These people skills you are developing will help you in your career. Your perspective will become more diversified, and you will develop strong interpersonal relationship skills that will be an asset to your future.

People matter! When you are going to college, your peers, professors, and friends matter. We don't have a crystal ball or know what is in the future. We cannot imagine who the person sitting next to us will become. Yes, even the person who snores next to you in class and the other one who eats the crunchiest chips at 8 o'clock in the morning will become someone worth knowing. Quite frankly, you might need those people one day. Hence, there is power in networking.

How do you network? By connecting with your peers and connecting with people of influence. We are most familiar with social media networking. For example, all of your friends on Facebook are part of your network. However, networking with professors and other professionals during college can help you get a job one day. Networking is basically communication within a group of people. It's reaching out to people to form a relationship—a bit like forming a friendship. Yes, the professor who puts you to sleep does know people. However, for networking to benefit you, you have to take initiative.

People won't remember you if you don't take initiative to be remembered!

When you are networking with professionals, your best position is to be a listener. These older, more established professionals have a lot of wisdom and experience to impart to you—wisdom and experience that could help shave some time from your college years. You don't have to tell these people all of your ambitions. Simply be willing to learn from their experiences and take the time to stay in contact with them.

If there were one thing I wish I would have done more of in college, it would be to have networked more. I did not realize the value of the connections I had made until after college when I needed them. It is a humbling experience to reconnect with people with whom you have lost touch. So stay connected. Doing so might require an occasional email, meeting, or lunch, but the long-term benefits outweigh the initial sacrifice. It is great knowing that people are supportive of you and want to help you. Networking generates more fans in the stands to cheer for you. Even if you are not outgoing, networking has enough value to make you force yourself to interact with people. Trust me, you will not be disappointed that you did.

For example, if a professor knows you are trying to get a job in Human Resources, they will be more willing to suggest an opportunity to you if they know you. One time, I was talking to a potential employer with a professor. When the professor gave me his stamp of approval, it made a big impact on the potential employer. The recommendation from someone else is really significant in getting a job.

Therefore, the message is clear: Value all your connections.

COLLEGE IN REAL LIFE

SUMMARY:

- Surround yourself with positive people who will influence you to be all that you can be.

- Avoid people who could potentially pull you away from your goal of graduating early.

- Get involved in campus activities that are fun and beneficial for your future.

- Take the initiative to network with peers and professors.

MAKE IT PRACTICAL:

1. Find a student organization on campus to get involved with.

2. Attend school-sponsored networking events with professionals.

3. Learn people skills by interacting with a diverse group of people.

CHAPTER THREE
Have Clear Goals

"A goal without a plan is just a wish."
– Antoine de Saint Exupery

College is a big investment—both financially and time wise. We're talking an investment of tens of thousands of dollars and at least two years of your life—maybe more. When so much is at stake, having a clearly defined goal—with a solid plan of action—is a must.

FAST TRACK TIP

If you simply say, "I want to graduate with my Bachelor's degree in two and a half years," but make no plans to reach that goal, chances are you won't achieve it. **Having a clearly defined goal—with a solid plan of action— is a must.**

Have you ever tried to get a group of people together without a plan? People end up here, there, and yonder, because it is difficult to communicate without a plan. For example, think of time when you and your friends wanted to go out for an evening of fun. If you simply said, "Let's go out and have fun," but nothing more, you probably spent the next hour with everyone saying, "Okay, what do you want to do?" "I don't know…what do you want to do?" It wasn't until someone stepped up and laid out the plan—"Let's grab a bite to eat at the diner, then go see that new movie, then play a game of pool"—that any real movement toward the ultimate goal of going out and having fun occurred.

The same is true of your college experience. If you simply say, "I want to graduate with my Bachelor's degree in two-and-a-half years," but make no plans to reach that goal, chances are you won't achieve it.

Goals and plans go hand-in-hand. Goals for life are important. Goals with a plan are effective.

THE IMPORTANCE OF GOALS

Goals should be broken down into short-term, long-term, and life goals. And each goal needs action steps or a plan to reach them, as there are small steps you can take every day to accomplish your goals over time.

> **SMART TALK**
>
> If you don't write your goals and plan down on paper, you are essentially just wishing something will happen someday… maybe. **Wishing is a very ineffective way to accomplish something.**

But don't just say your goals and plans aloud; you also have to write them down. Writing down your goals and plans is like putting your dreams into action. If you are going to try to remember your goals and plans without writing them down, the goal/plan won't last very long. It's too easy to forget.

If you don't write everything down on paper, you are essentially just wishing something will happen someday...maybe. Wishing is a very ineffective way to accomplish something. Ultimately, you will forget about your goals, and what you really want to accomplish may never happen. No one wants to live their whole life saying, "I never accomplished any of my goals." You would be miserable, cynical, and cranky.

Revising your goals and action steps over time is important too. You may realize that taking a different approach would be better or that you really need to be pursuing a different goal. Allow yourself permission to revise your list once or twice a year. Seasons of life change, and short-term goals can be affected.

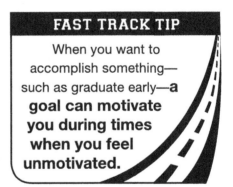

FAST TRACK TIP

When you want to accomplish something—such as graduate early—**a goal can motivate you during times when you feel unmotivated.**

How do goals affect your life? Goals enable you to have vision about the future. When you want to accomplish something, a goal can motivate you during times when you feel unmotivated. Goals are the propellers that move people to action.

Goals also help you stay on track when you have to make decisions. If you have to decide about work, travel, etc., your goals can help you make a decision that fits the direction of your life. But, if your only goal is to blow the biggest bubble in the whole world, you might need to expand your list.

GOAL SETTING BASICS

Your goals should include college, career, life, family, and personal goals. A good place to start is to ask yourself where you want to be in five years. Be creative. Then, write down goals for one year, two years, and five years.

In the one-year category, you could have goals to read a certain number of books, travel to a new place, or just finish a semester of school. Your goals don't have to be lofty. Then, you can break those goals down into months. What can you do each month to be one step closer to accomplishing your goal? Maybe you need to save a certain amount of money so you can go on that trip or do something else you have been looking forward to.

Whatever your goal is, it should be measurable and attainable. For example, reading a book a day for a whole year is a measurable goal, but not very attainable. Maybe a goal of reading a book every week or two weeks would be more attainable. Spending more time with your family is not a good goal either because it's not measurable. A better goal would be to have a family night scheduled once a week, which would enable you to spend more time with your family.

Remember, goals have to be more than "I want to be a better person." There is no way to measure becoming a better person. But if you break it down into specific things you want to be better at, you will be more likely to succeed.

Although this might all sound great to you, you're likely thinking that you have no goal or plan for today, nonetheless five years from now. To that I say, "Join the crowd. I have been there before."

When I first started college, I had goals for the one to two year range, but I could never figure out long-term goals. I remember sitting in my dad's office and him asking me where I wanted to be in five years. I just shrugged my shoulders. I had no idea. Five years seemed so far away, and goals seemed so permanent to me. How was I supposed to make goals for five years in the future when I could barely make it through that week?

SMART TALK

Give yourself permission to revise your goals, but never permission to go without goals or dreams.

But through my conversations with him, I learned that long-term goals do not have to be etched in stone. They are guidelines to help us stay on course and moving forward each and every day.

You can start dreaming today and setting goals for your future. Give yourself permission to revise your goals, but never permission to go without goals or dreams. Goals can be a propeller for your life, as sometimes, we just need something to push us forward.

Develop both short and long-term goals now, at the start of your college experience. Don't wait until after college. Although college life is busy, make time to think about your dreams, goals, and plans. It will help keep you from floundering while you're in college, as well as during your transition from college into the next stage of life. Having clear goals will help you during college when you are tempted to make dumb decisions. If your decision is going to negatively affect your life goals, don't do it. It won't be worth it. You don't have to have it all figured out...just keep dreaming!

SUMMARY:

- Goals are the propellers in life that move people to action.
- Goals should be measurable and attainable.
- Don't wait until after college. College is a great time to think about your dreams, goals, and plans.

MAKE IT PRACTICAL:

1. Make a list of your goals for the next year.
2. Write beside each goal a plan to accomplish it.
3. Put the list where you can see it every day.
4. Make another list of long-term goals.

CHAPTER FOUR
Hone Your Study Skills

"Success is the sum of small efforts,
repeated day in and day out."
– Robert Collier

now that you have started college, you may be thrilled. But do you remember the professor saying all that stuff about assignments and homework due at the next class? Does homework really start that soon? Yes. Since you only attend classes a few days a week rather than every day, you are responsible for doing assignments and studying for tests according to your syllabus.

Syllabus? What's that? It is a document your professor gives you on the first day of class, and it has a detailed description of the schedule for the semester, including tests, papers, and assignments. You will receive one for each class. Your syllabus is a very important piece of paper. Treat it like gold, as it will keep you on track all semester.

The syllabus will help you to know when and what to study. Studying is critical for getting good grades in college and graduating early.

PLAN YOUR STUDY TIME

The secret to successful studying is to make time to do it. Notice I said "make the time." Studying doesn't just happen. In order to pass tests, write papers, do assignments, and get out of college in less than four years, studying is unavoidable. Therefore, schedule ample time each week for studying.

SMART TALK

Studying doesn't just happen. Schedule ample time each week for studying.

Whatever you do, don't try to stay up all night studying for a test. Choose to study on your timetable rather than back yourself into a corner where the only option is to pull an all-nighter. Sure, everyone wants to hang out with friends, leaving studying as a second thought. However, if you revisit the original purpose of college, studying has to be a priority.

College requires you to implement the study habits you have already learned. However, during high school, your classes met more frequently than in college, and you received more detailed instruction from teach-

FAST TRACK TIP

Studying is critical for getting good grades in college and **graduating early.**

ers. As a result, it's quite possible that you never learned how to study effectively. If that's the case, here are a few tips on how to make studying most effective.

- **Make the commitment:** To be successful in your classes, you must commit to study time. Some classes will be more demanding than others. Since you will be balancing school, work, studying, friends, and family, you will be best served if you plan ahead. You can use a planner or a calendar on your computer to keep track of your schedule. When you are deciding on what time to study, make sure it is before 10 o'clock at night. When you stay up late or even all night to study, you are going to miss a lot of sleep, which puts you at risk of sleeping through the class you stayed up all night for. Talk about a waste of staying up all night!

- **Start early:** When you get an assignment or big project, start on it immediately.

While it might be tempting to do the easy parts of the project first, it's actually more beneficial to tackle the hardest and most time-consuming parts first. If you wait to do the hard parts last, you will ultimately procrastinate and dread it. However, when you start on the more complex aspects of a project, you will discover that you have plenty of time to put the finishing touches on it. Also, the easy stuff will be all that is left and you can quickly accomplish it. Therefore, start working on the project right away so you don't forget about it and panic the day it's due. Then, the day before it is due, you are simply printing it or submitting the project rather than frantically running around trying to get it done. College students talk about being stressed a lot. If you don't procras-

SMART TALK

For every credit hour, expect to study two to three hours per week. Translate that into a full-time semester of 15 credit hours, and you will be studying 30 to 40 hours a week!

tinate, you can avoid much stress and anxiety. When you have a project that is assigned for a whole semester, schedule it out the tasks you need to do each week to accomplish it. Whatever you do, don't put it off until the final week of classes. You will end up with one big headache if you do. Stay on schedule week-by-week and the project will be done before you know it.

- **Stay on top of homework:** When you sign up for college, you are not only enlisting yourself to go to class and pay attention; you are also signing up for all the class work in between the actual class times. Multiply the outside class work by four, five, or six classes, and your schedule is booked. It varies from class to class whether you're focusing on projects, papers, exams, or busywork, but they all have one thing in common: time. For every credit hour, expect to study two to three hours per week. Translate that into a full-time semester of 15 credit hours, and you will be studying 30 to 40 hours a week! That definitely requires your time and attention to succeed in the classes.

- **Read your textbooks:** I know, reading textbooks can be boring. But imagine sitting poolside, soaking up some rays, reading your textbook. Or...imagine sitting at a quaint outdoor café, drinking a latte, reading your textbook. In either scenario, it almost sounds like you're on vacation rather than studying, doesn't it? It certainly makes studying seem a little less dreadful. The point is that you don't have to be stuck in your room staring at the wall for hours "trying" to read your textbook.

Embrace the opportunity to choose your study location. Decide if you focus better in noisy or silent settings. Most of us have the perception that we must do homework in silence, but if you have the ability to focus despite noise, your locations are limitless. If you need a silent setting, go to a park and lay out a blanket and read, or find a library in your area that has a café or coffee shop to make the quiet experience more enjoyable.

If music, rather than overall noise, doesn't bother you, locate coffee shops or cafés with Wi-Fi. Then, you can download some classical music into your iPod and you can easily join the study crowd at coffee shops.

FAST TRACK TIP

Don't let others' lack of motivation determine your motivation. **Be motivated and stick with studying!**

Remember, in today's technological age, you can control where you study. You are no longer confined to one location. But the location you choose may significantly increase or decrease your level of satisfaction or frustration with school.

- **Switch it up:** Vary your study location frequently. In the same way that studying is monotonous and can be boring, going to the same place to study every day will sabotage your efforts to be productive, even if the same place is a local coffee shop. Whether you go to the library or a local coffee shop, find a place that enables you to concentrate. Some libraries also have individual study rooms you can reserve. If you are living on campus, your dorm room might not be the best place to study. Dorms tend to be loud and distracting. It always seems as if no one ever studies, and your friends often try to talk you out of studying. However, you can't let others' lack of motivation determine your motivation. Be motivated and stick with studying!

USE YOUR TEXTBOOK EFFECTIVELY

Most college classes require at least one textbook, sometimes more. Textbooks can be very expensive. Since they are not included in tuition fees, you must be prepared to pay for them yourself.

FAST TRACK TIP

There will be some things you will have to read completely... sometimes more than once to fully understand it. In that case, you have to **combine speed-reading and comprehension.**

When you are looking for textbooks, used textbooks are the best choice as they will save you a lot of money. Unfortunately, if the professor requires that you use the newest edition of the textbook, a used one may not be available. However, when you can choose, pick used textbooks every time. Whether the book is fresh off the press or has a few wrinkles or notes on the pages, it will serve the same purpose. Find a used textbook store in your community. If you don't have one in your area, find out the books you need and look for them online.

Also, ask your peers about classes they have taken. They might be willing to sell you a book directly. I have purchased and borrowed textbooks from friends many times. On a few occasions, I knew friends who had taken the class before but wanted to keep their textbook. They simply let me borrow the book, and I gave it back to them at the end of the semester. Talk about a win-win situation!

Half.com is a great place to look for used textbooks and a great place to sell books after you have used them. Of course, you can opt to keep your textbooks, but you may run out of space by the end of college. Therefore, keep only the textbooks you will actually use in the future.

I recommend you sell your books online or to a used bookstore after each semester. Textbooks are frequently updated by the publishers, and waiting until the end of the year could ruin your chances of selling your books.

Once you receive your textbook, you'll quickly find that carrying it gives you a good arm workout. But if you only learn how to carry your textbook, you will not benefit from it. You also need to learn how to read a textbook.

Since textbooks are usually as heavy as a couple of bricks and have tons of information crammed into them, it will be impossible for you to read every word in every textbook for four or five classes. If you tried to read everything, you could spend hours and hours every day just reading, not including assignments.

Yes, there will be some things you will have to read completely...sometimes more than once to fully understand it. In that case, you have to combine speed-reading and comprehension. Here's how you do that:

- Target the topic sentence of each paragraph.

- Then, scan the rest of the paragraph and read the final sentence in the paragraph.

- Once you comprehend the main concept, move on to the next paragraph.

When you are reading a textbook and taking notes, highlighting can help. Just use any colored highlighter and highlight the words or phrases in the book that seem most important to draw the main points out of the text. When you go back to review a chapter, you can focus on the highlighted parts to save time. If you buy a book that is already highlighted, no problem! Just use it to your advantage when you are studying.

Taking notes while you are reading can also be helpful. Although it might seem time consuming, you will probably save yourself time in the end by not having to re-read the material.

Take notes on the main ideas and supporting topics. Start by writing or typing the main topic and important details related to it. Continue doing this throughout the entire chapter. You are essentially making an outline of the chapter.

Taking notes is a little more extensive than just highlighting the book. So why should you take notes? Is it a waste of time? No, it will actually help you. By taking notes, you are able to remember information you have seen more than once. When you take good notes, you don't have to re-read your textbook, which will save time over the course of a semester.

Learning to highlight your textbook, take notes, and study will enable you to take more classes each semester without being overwhelmed. If you can take one more class each semester because of good study habits, you will be one step closer to graduating in less than four years.

As you learn the testing style of your professor, you will also discover the studying format that works best for that class. For example, if the professor tests on details, focus on details while you are reading. But if the professor focuses on broad concepts on tests, then study the overall concept and make the details secondary.

SMART TALK

As you **learn the testing style of your professor,** you will discover the studying format that works best for that class.

MAKE THE MOST OF CLASS TIME

If you take good notes during class, you're essentially making class time part of your study time. I was never a big note taker. To succeed, I had to make myself take notes because I knew it would help me in the end. Some of you might fall into the other extreme. You may feel compelled to write down every word the professor says. Falling into either extreme is not good. You don't have to write down every word, but you should write down the main ideas discussed or specific examples the professor gives.

Taking notes requires bringing paper or your computer to class. If you lose things easily, make sure your paper is in a spiral notebook.

When you need to study for a test, your notes are a great place to start. It can be difficult to memorize a bunch of material for a test. Therefore, apply the class information to real life examples while studying.

Additionally, make sure you go to class the day before an exam. Although it would seem like a good day to skip since you aren't covering new material, it really isn't a smart move.

Sitting in a class and going over the review of information can help you retain it for the test. Also, the professor might tell you additional information that is going to be on the test that they had not mentioned before. Sometimes they will talk about bonus points or open note opportunities. By going to class the day before the test, you are setting yourself up to succeed.

A FEW KEY WARNINGS

You are not in high school any longer. Now that you're in college, you have to take full responsibility for your academics. Here are two key points to remember:

- Professors are not going to babysit you through college. You will have to remember deadlines and test dates.

- Don't assume that just because they didn't tell you about a test that you don't have one. Read your syllabus and honor it.

While you are responsible for your academics, you can benefit from both studying by yourself and study groups. When you join a study group, make sure the people are actually interested in studying. The last thing you want is for your study group to become a coffee social. And remember that study groups do not replace doing your own work.

A common issue at all colleges today is plagiarism. The layman's definition of plagiarism is taking someone else's words and using them as your own. Since we live in the Internet age, students have access to all sorts of information. However, it is important that you avoid plagiarism. If you get caught, not only will it delay you from graduating early, but it may also completely end your college days.

Even if you use your own words but use someone else's idea, it is considered plagiarism if you do not give credit to the other person. There are serious consequences for plagiarism. It usually goes on your permanent record,

FAST TRACK TIP

Avoid plagiarism. If you get caught, not only will it delay you from graduating early, but it may also completely end your college days.

and/or you are suspended from the school. The price you have to pay for plagiarism is simply not worth it.

Most professors will submit papers to an online program that checks for plagiarism. It will be very apparent if you copy someone else's work or turn in a paper that is not your own. If you have any questions about it, ask your professor and avoid the mistakes of copying someone else's work.

A LITTLE HELP ALONG THE WAY

What happens if despite your best study efforts, you are failing a class? Even though you attend every class, take notes, and highlight your textbook, you still have no idea what's going on. Even worse, everyone around you seems to understand. It's as if the professor is speaking a foreign language and you have no interpreter.

Well, you do have access to an interpreter—he or she is known as a tutor.

When you are failing a class, you essentially have two options: withdraw from the class or get a tutor. If the class is required, you will have to retake it at some point. So before you drop the class, find someone who can help you.

Check to see if your school has a tutoring department or if there is a graduate student who could tutor you. The reason you are failing might be the misunderstanding of a simple concept. Also, you could talk to your professor about it. They might know someone who could help you if they do not have time outside of class to tutor you.

No one can deny that college is harder than high school. The class format is different and can be difficult, depending on your preferred learning style. Usually, the professors move quickly through the material with the assumption that everyone understands. The sooner you get help, the better off you will be. Don't pretend the problem doesn't exist. Face up to the problem and do something about it.

By honing your study skills, using your resources effectively, and getting help when you need it, you can get through college quickly and easily.

COLLEGE IN REAL LIFE

SUMMARY:

- In order for studying to be a priority, you are going to have to "make" time to do it.

- Switch up the location when you are studying. It will be less boring and tedious.

- Do not plagiarize. Give credit to others for their words and ideas.

RESOURCES:

- Half.com offers used textbooks at a discounted price.

- BarnesandNoble.com/Textbooks allows you to "rent" textbooks and return them.

- Amazon.com/Textbook-Buyback enables you to sell your textbooks to Amazon.com for a gift card.

MAKE IT PRACTICAL:

1. Get your booklist for your classes.
2. Look up the books online by the ISBN number found on the back of the book.
3. Buy used textbooks.
4. Take your books to your classes.

CHAPTER FIVE

Shave Time with CLEP Tests and Summer School

"Opportunity is missed by most people because it is dressed in overalls and looks like work."
– *Thomas Edison*

another secret to fast tracking your education is the College-Level Examination Program, also known as CLEP tests. These are not usually highly publicized, so you have to ask about them. It's a standardized test for a specific subject area that uses a pass/fail scoring system. CLEP tests can be beneficial to students who have a higher aptitude in different areas of study. Fortunately, you do not have to be a genius to pass a CLEP test. That is good news for most of us. But you do have to be willing to study beforehand and not rely solely on what you know.

A variety of CLEP tests are available. Some are based on general subjects like math, science, or history, while others are more specific, such as Spanish, microeconomics, or marketing. The subjects you can CLEP out of are classes you would generally take in the first two years of college.

If you want to take a CLEP test, you need to find out if your school offers them. If your school does not offer CLEP tests, many times they will offer placement tests, where you receive the credits for the classes below the class in which you

FAST TRACK TIP

Investigate your CLEP test options. **They can save you much time and money.**

place. In order to find out about CLEP tests, ask your admissions counselor about them. Usually, if you search a university website, they will have information online.

Being aware that CLEP tests exist gives you more options. However, if you think the test is going to be easy, you may be surprised. They are challenging and they do reveal what you know. If you do not know enough material to pass the test with a score of 51, you don't get the credits for the class. The broader courses seem to be more challenging because they cover a larger range of information, including paintings, sculptors, science equations, etc.

I first learned about CLEP tests through my sister. When she was enrolling in college, her admissions counselor told her about them. Since I was going to attend the same school, I was immediately interested. After she took a CLEP test and passed it, I began to think that I might be able to do it too. I certainly didn't want to take a class that I could test out of and save time and money.

THE DOLLARS AND CENTS OF CLEP TESTS

When you compare tuition to the cost of the CLEP test, you will be surprised. For example, a CLEP test typically costs $70 or $80, while tuition at my school was $400 per credit hour. That means a three-hour course cost $1,200. If I took a CLEP test for that course and passed, I'd be saving over $1,000. Since I was trying to control the cost of school, I was willing to take the risk.

If you are a decent test taker, trying a CLEP test is worth it. If you don't pass, you are out $80 or so, but if you pass, you save $1,000 or more plus the time of not having to take the class. That's not a bad deal.

But please don't go into the test blindly, as then you'd be wasting both your time and money. Instead, buy a study guide at a local bookstore and spend some time studying and reviewing the information. Although you may want to buy

FAST TRACK TIP

When you are starting college, you want to **take classes you are interested in.** Since CLEP tests are mainly general education courses, you can skip those classes and jump right into taking the classes you want to take.

a textbook to study, I never found that helpful. If you use a study guide, you actually have practice reviewing the information in a test format. The cost of the study guide is definitely worth the price.

IMAGINE THE POSSIBILITIES

Since I knew CLEP tests were an option, I planned my class schedule my freshman year with the test in mind. If I could CLEP a class, I didn't need to enroll in it.

Realize, though, that not every school will offer CLEP tests, even though it is a nationally standardized test. Ask your school if they offer the test. If they do not, don't give up. If the school takes CLEP test credits, then you can take the test at a local testing center. Don't be afraid to ask questions.

Imagine with me…You have to take only one test for a particular class—a CLEP test. You can save a lot of time by not having to sit through class for three hours a week for a semester, not having to take tests, not having to do projects, and not having to complete homework. You don't have to take that class at all; you can take another class in its place. When you are starting college, you want to take classes you are interested in. Since CLEP tests are mainly general education courses, you can skip those classes and jump right into taking the classes you want to take.

My first experience taking a CLEP test was nerve-wracking. The test was offered in the records and registration office at the university. They took me to a back room with a computer in it. I sat in that room, at the computer, by myself for an hour and a half. I answered each question the computer screen displayed. There was a timer on the screen so I could pace myself through the questions. Finally, that last question appeared. I knew that once I answered it my score would show immediately.

I sat there covering my eyes with my hands. My heart was pounding; sweat dripped down my forehead. I knew that the moment I opened my eyes, I would find out if the study time and test fee were worth it. Although I wanted to know, I didn't want to know at the same time. The anticipation was almost unbearable. I pulled my fingers apart, anticipating the dreaded. I was a basket full of nerves. Lo and behold, the computer screen was smiling at me. I had passed! My mind started racing. I had passed a three-hour college class—a class I would have had to sit through for an entire semester—in a matter of an hour and a half, and for only $80. Unbelievable!

Looking back, I know it was not necessary to be so nervous. However, I did learn about the process of taking the CLEP test. You can take a relaxed approach to taking CLEP tests. You will know before you leave whether you pass or fail. And no one is going to laugh at you if you don't pass. By calming your nerves before you begin the test, your mind will be able to focus better.

After I had passed the first test, I was so excited. There was a moment when I realized how beneficial it could be overall. I immediately started looking at other CLEP test options and began planning the "how" part of taking CLEP tests, as some tests have to be taken before you take a certain number of credits.

Realistically, you can probably take one or two CLEP tests per semester. One per semester is a good place to start. If you want to take two, I would recommend taking one at the start of the semester and the second immediately after the semester's final exams are over. CLEP tests are supposed to help you, not overwhelm you. If you don't have adequate time to prepare, you will have additional stress in your life. Preparation is key.

If you fail the CLEP test, you are out the cost of the test. However, you will have gained valuable experience and will be better able to gauge your ability to take other tests. You can take the test again at a later time; check with your advisor for the current wait time rules. If you don't pass the CLEP test the second time, just take the class. You will probably learn something in it.

Everyone is stronger in different areas. If you have always struggled with science classes, taking a science CLEP test would not be the best idea. But if you've always been strong in English, you might want to take an English CLEP test. If you fail a CLEP test even though you are usually strong in that subject area, it may just mean you struggle at test taking, which is okay. Whether or not you pass a CLEP test does not determine your intelligence. Some people are just more familiar with the subject and are good at taking tests. If you fail two or more CLEP tests, accept your limitations and determine to enjoy taking the classes.

I received 29 credits by taking CLEP tests. That is a whole year of college! If you do the math on it one more time, I saved over $10,000 by taking CLEP tests. While there isn't a set standard of how many hours you can CLEP, you can only take the maximum CLEP tests offered, which is approximately 30 tests. Timing is everything, because you have to take general CLEP tests before you have 60 hours of college credit. That means you need to take them within your first two years. However, since subject tests are more specific, you just have to take them before you graduate. Once you take the test, it will go on your transcript as a pass, and the credit counts toward your degree.

If you have a goal of graduating in less than four years, CLEP tests can help you. Even if you don't want to CLEP as many credits as I did, what if you received three or six credits? That would save you half a semester of time and work. Start thinking. Anything is possible.

Remember, the secret to graduating early is planning. You can have all the good intentions in the world about graduating early, but without planning, it will be difficult to accomplish.

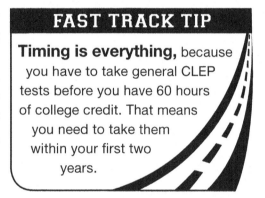

FAST TRACK TIP

Timing is everything, because you have to take general CLEP tests before you have 60 hours of college credit. That means you need to take them within your first two years.

If you take CLEP tests, your program of study might be a little different than the typical freshman. With that being said, there are some classes that everybody has to take. Just take the exceptions into consideration when scheduling classes. If you decide to take CLEP tests before you start college, you will be way ahead.

SUMMER SCHOOL

After you finish your first year of classes, you may be considering summer school. For most freshmen, the idea of summer school is intimidating. They are ready for a break and are simply glad they survived their first year of college.

FAST TRACK TIP

Summer school is a great way to catch up or get ahead on your degree.

However, summer school is a good option if you want to catch up on classes or want to graduate early.

Unlike regular semester classes, summer school classes are fast pace. You have a shorter amount of time to do the course work, and you have to attend class more frequently.

For example, if your summer class is four weeks long, you attend class for three hours a day, every day, for four weeks. Sound terrible? It really isn't because you only have to go to that class for a month.

Some people like the fast pace of summer school and some people don't. It all depends on whether you prefer to learn over a longer period of time. If you are able to quickly engage and comprehend concepts, summer school is a good option.

I liked taking summer school classes. It was a quick and easy way for me to get a couple of extra classes per year. My sister, on the other hand, didn't like summer school. Since summer school classes aren't "required," enrolling over the summer is a decision of personal preference.

The advantage of summer school is that you can concentrate on only one or two classes instead of juggling multiple classes like you do during a regular semester. Be aware that some classes simply won't work as well during summer, such as a foreign language class, where you need to be immersed in the language for a longer period of time to truly understand it. Also, some courses are not offered in the summer. Talk with your advisor if you are uncertain.

If you need an extra class, summer school is a great way to catch up or get ahead on your degree. Additionally, if you are concerned about enjoying your summer, take a class that lasts only four or five weeks instead of eight or nine weeks. Then, it won't last all summer.

IT'S NEVER TOO LATE TO START

Maybe you are reading this information and you are halfway through college. You have taken a lot of unnecessary classes, you don't know what direction to study, and basically you are lost in the college process. Here's some good news: you can start planning now! Yes, you may have taken classes that you don't need, but you don't have to continue in that pattern. Determine today to be an initiator in your college education.

It is key that you don't go to meetings with academic advisors unprepared. Have a plan that you can discuss with an academic advisor. They are there to tell you the order in which classes must be taken and to give general guidelines. Let go of the time you have lost and determine to move forward with a new plan.

Now, you might be the type of person who plans nothing. So planning for college would go against the grain for you.

If that is you, find someone—an advisor, sibling, student mentor, etc.—who can help you in the planning process. Just because you are not a "planner" does not mean you can't graduate early. Most schools require that you meet with an advisor before you schedule classes. If you have a basic plan, most advisors are willing to work with you to help you accomplish your educational goals. You can make a plan for college without being a planner in other areas of your life.

SUMMARY:

- CLEP tests save you time and money. You can receive credit for a college class by taking a test.

- CLEP tests are a secret to graduating from college early. However, you have to study for it before you take the test!

- Summer school is a great way to catch up or get ahead on your degree.

RESOURCES:

- ClepExamPracticeTests.com offers sample questions for CLEP tests.

- 4tests.com offers practice tests for CLEP tests.

MAKE IT PRACTICAL:

1. Ask your advisor if your school offers CLEP test.

2. Decide on a CLEP test to take.

3. Buy a study guide online or at a bookstore.

4. Study for four to six weeks.

5. Take the test. Good luck!

CHAPTER SIX
Choose Your Major

"Without passion, you don't have energy; without
energy, you have nothing. Nothing great in the world has
been accomplished without passion."
– Donald Trump

think of those people you know who really love their job. They are always talking about it and are excited about going to work. Now, think about those people you know who hate their job. They complain about it and are always saying negative things about their co-workers. And, if they admitted it, their hatred for what they are doing is affecting all aspects of their life.

If you start working 40 hours a week when you are 22 years old and work until you are 60, that is about 75,000 hours of your life spent at work. Who wants to be miserable that much of the time? Hence, it is important to discover your passion to pursue a career you will enjoy.

CHOOSE WISELY

Everyone wants to know that they have chosen the right thing to do in life. But with so many choices, it is hard to

Realize that your major is just a starting point, as most people have different jobs throughout the course of their life. So just because you major in an area does not mean you'll be working in that field forever.

be confident about your decision. Fortunately, many books and resources are available to help you discover your interests and strengths.

The key is to choose a major that you enjoy and that you have a natural bent toward. Then, be confident about your decision. Realize that your major is just a starting point, as most people have different jobs throughout the course of their life. So just because you major in an area does not mean you'll be working in that field forever.

I've found that most stress about deciding on a major is self-inflicted. College students often feel as if they have to know today what they are going to do with their lives for the next 40 years. That is just not true. The further you walk down the road, the more clarity you will have about your decision. However, if you feel so uneasy about your decision that you can't sleep at night, talk with an advisor or friend. Maybe it would be good for you to change your direction. Have the courage to evaluate where you are and do something about it.

When you are trying to decide on a major, it is easy to feel stuck. Your perception is that everyone else knows what he or she wants to do, and you are the only one who doesn't. I have news for you. Half of the people who decide on a major before they start college will probably change it at least once before they finish. So there is no need to be worried.

GET UNSTUCK

If you are really stuck in deciding on a major, the following are a few questions to ask yourself before moving forward.

- **If you could do anything with your life and money wasn't an issue, what would you do?** This is a great place to start. We can all answer this question with something. What is that one thing? Maybe you would be a photographer, a marine biologist, a life coach, a songwriter, or a number of other things. I have found that when you ask people this question, most people have an answer. It might not come to mind right away, so take some time to think about it. What is that one thing for you? It might be something you have never told anyone before.

- **How does the dream fit with your life?** Does your dream align with your natural gifts or your lifestyle? For example, if you want to be a veterinarian but are severely allergic to animals, then that dream might not be an option. It is a realistic dream, but it wouldn't be a good fit for a person with allergies. However, maybe you could work with marine life instead. Once you have a starting block, you can build on it. If you have some place to start, it is easier to find areas of study in which you are interested.

- **At what points in your life did you feel accomplished, fulfilled, and fully alive?** For you, the moments might have been in your childhood or just last week. What moments stand out in your mind? You might be thinking, "What in the world?" Just go with it. Did you feel fulfilled when you were in your first play in grade school? Maybe it was when you won the spelling bee in the 5th grade. Was it when you scored the winning goal in the state championship game? You can check the resource section at the end of the chapter for other self-discovery questionnaires.

- **How are those moments related to your dream?** Find connection points. What activity were you doing when you felt fulfilled or accomplished? If you nursed a bird back to health and helped your brother after he broke his arm, then your dream to be a doctor connects with your sense of accomplishment and passion for helping others. What is the common theme or themes in your life?

- **What are you really passionate about?** What makes you get really excited or mad? You might think that is an odd question. But if something really upsets you, such as when you hear about children dying from preventable diseases, you should write it down. What topic can you get started on and not stop talking about? Your passion, dream, and natural aptitude should all collide in your area of interest.

Maybe you have never thought about these questions before. If not, that's okay; you can start thinking about them now. Usually, the "thing" we are supposed to do in life directly relates to what we want to do and what we are good at. That seems pretty simple to figure out. Choosing a major and figuring out your career doesn't have to cause you undue stress. What do you like to do? Are you good at it? How can you use that activity or those skills to benefit you in a future career? Sometimes the process seems difficult to navigate, but by focusing on these simple questions, it doesn't have to be.

NO MORE FLOUNDERING

Recently, I was talking with a gentleman who works at a chain coffee shop. He is in his mid-thirties, a college graduate, and still doesn't know what he wants to do when he "grows up." I applaud him for having a job, but you

FAST TRACK TIP

If you are going to invest time into studying something, **study something you enjoy and something employable.**

don't have to spend your whole life floundering between jobs, never knowing if what you are doing is right.

"Floundering" refers to those people who have a "no job, don't know what to do, and don't care" attitude after they graduate from college...and sometimes for many years after. You have probably seen the floundering people before. I know I have, and it is easy to fit that bill if you have no plan. The only way to avoid floundering is by moving forward. Discovering who you are and your interests before you graduate college will help you avoid floundering as well.

For example, an Olympic gymnast will not be able to compete her entire life. Being a gymnast is right for now, but as she ages, her abilities and interests will change. She may become a coach, own a gym, or pursue a completely different interest. The key is that she has identified an interest and can see a progression of occupations in the future. So if you are going to invest time into studying something, please study something you enjoy and something employable. If you study literature because you like to read but have no ambition to work in publishing, a library, a museum, or a writing field, then you need to re-evaluate your decision. Floundering is inevitable if you make no decision or a half-hearted decision.

REAL WORLD EXPERIENCE

The process of discovering your passion has begun; run with it! After you have decided on a major, there are many different career paths within one major. For example, if you decide to get a business degree, there are accounting, economics, management, marketing, or Human Resources careers. Within those categories, there are many jobs for which you could prepare. When you decide on a major, explore the different job options within your field.

Now that you are headed in a direction, you can gain practical experience through a process called job shadowing.

Job shadowing is following a professional for a day at their job. It is not a big commitment—just one day to experience life on the job. Most people are more than willing to let students shadow them and to share their expertise. To find a professional to shadow, check with your college advisor. Sometimes they have connections with people in your field of interest. When you are scheduling a job shadow, call to confirm the day before. Occasionally things come up and the professional cannot do it on the pre-determined day. Calling the day before to confirm will minimize a change in plans.

A more in-depth look at a job could involve an internship, which is an opportunity to work in a company while still in school so you can gain work experience. Internships can be either paid or unpaid. Although it would seem that an unpaid internship would be a waste of your time, you could still gain valuable work experience that would look great on your résumé! Better to waste your time on an internship than to waste years on a career you hate.

Sometimes the initial sacrifice of pay can greatly benefit you down the road, as the company you are interning for might offer you a job. Therefore, don't underestimate the power of doing your best no matter what the pay.

Internships are a great way to become familiar with actual jobs in your field that are not typical. Recently, I was talking with a college student who loved geography but didn't know what to do with a geography degree. He found out about a Geospatial Sciences major, which would allow him to work with maps to create things such as GPS devices. This is one example of a non-typical major that is employable.

Finally, check to see when a "job fair" is coming to your school. Usually, companies that are hiring for jobs or internships will come to the job fair and talk with students about the different opportunities at their company. This is a great way to network with business professionals in your field and even get an interview. Inquire about the job placement rate for graduates in your field. The job placement rate is the number of graduates who become employed after graduating in a particular field of study.

BE ALL YOU CAN BE

There is usually a lot of pressure to decide on a major before you start college. Rest assured that you do not have to decide on a major before you start school. It is completely okay to not know exactly what you are going to do with your life when you walk onto your college campus. The discovery of your passion, dream, and natural aptitude will

FAST TRACK TIP

While trying various majors may broaden your horizons, it will also keep you in school for a long time. **Don't rush making your decision** and you'll have a better idea of what to decide.

help you in making a great career decision.

If you do declare a major and hate it, you can change it. It will be best if you can change it in the first two years of school so you don't invest too much time into major-specific classes. If you have already taken a substantial number of classes in one area, maybe you could make it a minor and choose another major. I would not recommend jumping around, trying multiple majors. While trying various majors may broaden your horizons, it will also keep you in school for a long time. Remember that you have to take those classes you are trying for an entire semester. That means you are going to lose a lot of time "trying" them out. If you don't rush making your decision, you will have a better idea of what to decide.

Once I chose a major, I stuck with it. Fortunately, I didn't waste time on classes I didn't need. However, I still stressed over my decision. I remember sitting in a class, distraught about my major. I didn't know what I wanted to do with a business degree, and I liked other classes outside of business. My professor talked with me after class and gave me two key insights that day: 1) There are professors that really care about students, and 2) I had gotten so worked up about it all that I just needed a little perspective.

As it turned out, I was worried about all the wrong things. My professor and I talked through all of my options, and she encouraged me to get a minor in a different area that I was interested in. It was great advice, and I followed it. So if you feel distraught about your major, talk to someone about it. They can give you perspective and advice on what to do moving forward. Sometimes we are not as far off track as it seems to us. That is good news!

I really enjoyed psychology and communications, so I decided to get an "applied communications" minor. It's a communications focus that is more about interpersonal relationships and group communication instead of the technical aspects of communications studies. I loved going to classes and learning about group dynamics and people, and it was complimentary to what I was already studying in business. I also got to interact with different people by stepping outside of my major. It was a stretching experience all over again.

I had to do a radio workshop as part of my minor. Although I had grown up around radio and media, working a shift on the school radio station each week was a new experience. I also had to be part of a drama team for a semester. If it weren't required, I would have never done it. But it stretched me in my ability to communicate in front of an audience, and I met some great people through it.

Sometimes it is good to stretch yourself outside of your comfort zone. Learning to stretch and grow is an art. If you decide on a major and are being stretched to the point of breaking, reconsider. But, if it is causing you to grow through being stretched, that's great!

COLLEGE IN REAL LIFE

SUMMARY:

- If you start working 40 hours a week when you are 22 years old and work until you are 60, that is about 75,000 working hours. Choose a career you enjoy.

- Your career should be a collision of your passion, interests, and accomplishments.

- Internships and job shadowing are a great way to gain job experience.

RESOURCES:

- Career Quiz (http://www.careerpath.com/career-tests/career-quiz/)

- StrengthsQuest.com – Here you can purchase a book to discover your strengths.

MAKE IT PRACTICAL:

1. Write down the things you enjoy doing and the accomplishments that have brought satisfaction to you.

2. Think about what you would do if money weren't an issue.

3. Make a connection with your interest and a possible career.

4. Job shadow a professional in that field.

5. Apply for an internship.

CHAPTER SEVEN
Money Matters

"It's not your salary that makes you rich;
it's your spending habits."
— Charles A. Jaffe

money, money, money. Everyone needs money. We require money to live, to have fun, and to eat. Therefore, you need to know how to handle money. A secret to succeeding in college, especially when you're on the fast track, is being responsible with your money.

The first step is to get a bank account. You can deposit checks from your job into your account so you don't have cash lying around. Pick a bank that is convenient. If you are going to school in another city, you could pick a bank that is local to you now as well as to your hometown. When you go to the bank, request to open a personal checking account. These accounts are usually free to open; you simply have to make

FAST TRACK TIP

A secret to succeeding in college, especially when you're on the fast track, is **being responsible with your money.**

an initial deposit into the account. Some banks even give you your first box of checks free.

Most banks have an online banking option, which makes keeping track of your account(s) convenient. You can view your transactions and money in your account in real time by using online banking. You can set this up when you set up your account. Then, you will be able to access your bank account at any time via a computer or mobile device. Just make sure that it is a secure Internet connection to avoid fraud.

Once you fill out the paperwork, you will be given a debit card, temporary checks, and deposit slips. But don't have a party just yet because you have a piece of plastic. Debit cards and credit cards are not the same.

DEBIT VERSUS CREDIT

When you use a debit card, you are directly paying for something out of your bank account. Therefore, you must have money in your account to be able to buy something. If you don't have money, don't buy things!

SMART TALK

When you use a debit card or write a check, you are directly paying for something out of your bank account. Therefore, **you must have money in your account to buy something.**

When you buy something and don't have enough money to cover the purchase, you will be charged an overdraft fee. Now, not only do you have to pay the overdraft fee of $25 or more, but you also have to pay the amount you overdrew. For example, you buy a shirt for $15 but only have $10 in your account. You overdrew your account by $5. You will then have to pay the $5 plus the $25 overdraft fee. That shirt just cost you $40.

Additionally, the blank checks you receive from the bank are directly linked to your bank account. You have to have money in your account so your checks don't "bounce." Checks work the same way as a debit card; you will be charged overdraft fees if your bank account does not have enough money in it. So as you can see, it's important that you are aware of your account balance at all times.

Credit cards are different. You can charge things to your credit card up to the credit limit the company gives you. Then, the credit card company will send you a bill at the end of each month stating how much you owe. This is where credit cards get dangerous. If you spend money you don't have, you are not going to be able to pay off the balance at the end of the month. You can pay less than you owe, but whatever amount you leave unpaid on the credit card will be subject to an interest fee. So now you're not only paying back what you charged—you're also paying a certain percentage extra to the credit card company. Doing this for one month may not seem like a big deal; however, when you do this month after month and keep charging more and more to the credit card, you can quickly get buried in debt.

> **SMART TALK**
>
> "If your output exceeds your income, **then your upkeep will be your downfall.**"
> –R.C. Amer

My dad once said, "If your output exceeds your income, then your upkeep will be your downfall." In other words, when you are trying to buy a bunch of clothes or eat out all the time, you will probably exceed your income. Then, your friends will think you can continue to spend money with them. To maintain that popular status, you feel that you have to keep using your credit card. Then, you will have so much debt that you won't be able to pay it; hence, your downfall. You have to be able to live on your income only, not on credit.

Credit card companies will try very hard to get you to "buy-in" to their product. They will send you applications and credit cards in the mail. They will offer you rewards and incentives for signing on the dotted line. Don't give in. Just throw the advertisements and marketing materials in the trash.

"But they already have my name engraved on the credit card," you might say. So what! It is just a marketing ploy to make you use it. If you don't have enough money to support yourself, get a job. A lifestyle of debt is no way to start your life.

Credit card companies do not care about you...plain and simple. They just want to make money from the interest you have to pay. Despite what their marketing messages might say, credit cards are not there to help you; they are a business for the credit card company to make money. Don't be naive.

Many times, schools will offer credit cards on campus. Companies will come in and set up a booth or a table to promote credit cards to students. They are usually giving away something free, like clothes or food. This marketing can be enticing for students. "I'll get the card now to get the free stuff and just cancel later," many think. But that is not realistic thinking. Just say "no" before you have the card in your hand. It will be easier to say "no" then instead of when you want to buy something.

BUDGET RESPONSIBLY

Money is often a struggle for college students and their parents. Many fights stem from not having any money or using money unwisely. A couple hundred dollars is not worth ruining your relationship with your parents. So be responsible with your finances. Everyone wants to grow up, but many don't want to be responsible. Unfortunately, growing up and responsibility go hand-in-hand. If you want to be treated like an adult, you have to act like one. Being responsible with your money is a great place to start.

> **SMART TALK**
>
> Everyone wants to grow up, but many don't want to be responsible. Unfortunately, **growing up and responsibility go hand-in-hand.**

First, live within your means. This will mean having a budget. Don't cringe yet. A budget is basically a plan you use to spend your money wisely. By having and following a solid budget, you should have enough money to pay the bills that are most important and still have something left over. Learning to manage your money will help you long-term.

When should you start your budget? Right now! Whenever you start getting paid, whether that money comes from a job or from your parents, you need a budget to know how to spend, save, and give. It is important to make a realistic budget rather than an idealistic one. We all have ideals about how much money we would like to make and how we would like to spend it. But your budget will only be helpful if you base it on your current income.

People get stressed when they know they don't have enough money and even when they have no idea about their finances. And if you're trying to graduate college early, additional stress from money issues is the

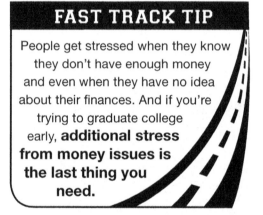

FAST TRACK TIP

People get stressed when they know they don't have enough money and even when they have no idea about their finances. And if you're trying to graduate college early, **additional stress from money issues is the last thing you need.**

last thing you need. Budgets aren't restricting; they relieve the stress of the unknown. When you follow a budget, you won't have to wonder if you can make it this month; you will know exactly where you are financially.

So now let's discuss how to make a budget. This applies to everyone—both traditional and non-traditional students. If you have never made a budget, today is the day! It is not difficult; just follow the guidelines I outline.

I have created the **3N Budget Method** to help you. Your budget will be divided into three categories:

• **Non-negotiable items** – these include your costs for housing, utilities, and food

- **Necessary items** – these include savings, auto insurance, gas, and health insurance

- **Negotiable items** – these include cell phone bill, TV/Internet bill, entertainment, and clothes

For many people, the negotiable category is a challenge. They lose sight of the fact that they really can live without some of life's luxuries. Face it, TV, a cell phone, and even the Internet are luxuries, not necessities. These items simply make life more comfortable or convenient.

If you have expenses that are not mentioned, add them to the appropriate category. If it is a traveling/adventure category, put it in the negotiable category.

To begin, start looking at your non-negotiable items. How can you possibly trim these expenses? If you live by yourself, maybe you could find a roommate to decrease the cost of housing. Maybe you can limit how many times a week you eat out. You have to allocate money for food, but maybe you can stretch your food dollars by buying staple items such as cereal in larger quantities and even using coupons. You can find coupons for food online or in a Sunday newspaper.

Put your money into the non-negotiable items first. The money that is left can be applied to the necessary items. Don't forget to try to cut back on necessary items as well. Your car needs gas to drive to school, but could you carpool with a friend a couple days a week? Also, if you live close to campus, perhaps you could ride your bike to save money on gas.

Then, take the leftover money and put it toward your negotiable items. I admit, these can be tricky. If you have been used to Internet, a cell phone, and TV, it will be hard to let one of these go. But maybe you don't have to completely eliminate any of them. For example, instead of having Internet on your phone, perhaps you could buy a basic cell phone plan to save money. If you can use the Internet at school, maybe you can not have it at your apartment. Good budget decisions will help you be prepared for unexpected expenses and give you more money for an occasional treat.

Before you clinch your fist and refuse to do a budget, give it a full-fledged run for three months. Notice how things change and how you will become more cautious about spending your money on frivolous things.

Also, you can use online programs to track your spending. Mint.com connects with your bank account to let you know your spending habits in real time.[1] There are also apps available for your phone. You can set limits on your spending and do a detailed budget within these technology tools. Just because you have never made a budget doesn't mean that you can't. Once you have made a budget, it is easy to make occasional changes.

Finally, integrating a budget into your life is the most important step. A plan without action is worthless. Some common excuses for not following a budget are as follows:

- I am bad with numbers.

- I don't make very much money.

- I make too much money, so a budget doesn't matter.

- It's too hard to stay on track.

- I will never be able to do anything I want ever again.

All of those excuses have no base in reality. In fact, they are even more reason to make a budget. If you are bad with numbers, you need a budget! When you spend $5 on a burger, then $10 on a pizza, followed by everyone going mini-golfing and getting ice cream for $15, your expenses add up quickly. Don't be caught off guard. Today can be a new day for you and a budget is a great place to start.

BE PREPARED

In addition to day-to-day expenses, you need to be prepared for emergencies too. When your computer crashes, you break your arm, or your car is stranded in the middle of nowhere, you need to have an emergency fund. Rather than always calling your parents when you are in a bind, you need an emergency fund to deal with the unexpected.

Emergencies happen to everyone. It is hard to prepare for them, hence the term "emergency." Before you flip the page and ignore this section, know that this is for you. Everyone needs to have $500 to $1,000 set aside in an emergency fund. How do you get that money? Well, working for it is a great way.

SMART TALK

Your emergency account should be a separate savings account that you don't touch for daily expenses. Remember, **needing money for chips and soda is NOT an emergency.**

Fund your emergency account as fast as you can. Once you use money from your emergency fund to cover an expense, re-plenish it. Your emergency account should be a separate savings account that you don't touch for daily expenses. Remember, needing money for chips and soda is NOT an emergency.

In addition to your emergency fund, you should have a long-term savings fund or savings account. Plan to save at least 10% of your income. If you can save more, you will be ahead. For example, if you make $1,000 per month, save $100 per month. Even if you make only $100 per month, plan to save $10. Start saving as early as possible and you will develop a great habit. Your saved money will add up over time.

You can get a savings account at your bank to keep this money separate from your checking account. It's too dif-ficult to keep track of your savings and spending money if they are in the same account. Therefore, I highly recom-mend that you have a separate savings account that you put money into every month.

Once you have a sizeable amount in savings, you will want to consider investing your money to make it grow. It's never too early to think about your future, so consider opening an IRA account.

You might even consider giving 10% of your income to a charity or your church as well. The principle of the farmer remains true. You reap what you sow. If you sow generosity, you will in turn receive it. No matter your religious affiliation, generosity will always come back to you. What is a project you could adopt that would help someone else? Maybe you could give a child a year of food and education through a child-sponsorship program.

You may be someone who needs to make just a few changes to get on track financially, or you may need a financial overhaul. Wherever you fall in the spectrum, initiate change in your situation. If you need a financial overhaul, allow a budget to change your spending habits. Keep track of the money you are spending, whether cash or using

> ## SMART TALK
>
> Although our culture spends and spends, if you want to have money, you are going to have to save. **Be wise in how you use money.**

your debit card. If you are having trouble staying within your budget, start using only cash. If you don't have the actual money, then you can't spend it. This might sound extreme, but if you spend more money than you earn, you will never be debt-free. Although our culture spends and spends, if you want to have money, you are going to have to save. I have yet to find money growing on trees. Be wise in how you use money.

But remember, a budget is just a structure. It is like the blueprint for a house. The house isn't built until the blueprint is put into action. You have to put the budget into action and commit to following it. Otherwise, nothing will change. Until you make a budget and stick to it, you will be nagged by the uncertainty of your finances. Don't let money, or lack of money, control you.

STUDENT LOAN DEBT

Student loans are a form of debt that you carry with you for many years. When you are paying minimum payments, which is typically what the loan companies encourage, the amount of money you are paying on interest is ridiculous. Unfortunately, student loans have become so common that people live with them, like a ball and chain wrapped around their neck, for years. Does that really sound like fun?

I am here to give you a little insight about student loans. Student loans have become a trend. It's as if they are the new brand of clothing, and everyone is crazed about them. Companies that of-

FAST TRACK TIP

When you have a lot of debt, it limits your options, career choices, and goals after you graduate from college. Your dreams, goals, and desires are limited by a financial payment.

fer student loans make it sound like the ideal way to pay for school. However, it is not. Student loans have been around for a while, but more and more students are using them to pay for school. Before you read any further, understand that you don't have to be one of those people.

It's natural for you and your parents to wonder how much your college education is going to cost. With the cost of college rising, student loans seem to be the only option. Realize, though, that loans are not your only option. They shouldn't even be an option!

Consider this: If you borrow $60,000 for school, payback is coming. You are going to have a large payment of $600 to $800 every month after you graduate for 20 or more years. Yes, student loans can linger for a long time. Even after people are married, have a house, start a family, and change professions a few times, many are still paying for their education 15 or 20 years later. So the question is, "Is there another way to pay for college?"

SMART TALK

When it comes to paying for college, **student loans are not your only option.** In fact, they shouldn't even be an option!

Yes.

You might be wondering how. If I had college debt, I wouldn't be sitting here writing this book. When you have a lot of debt, it limits your options, career choices, and goals after you graduate from college. Your dreams, goals, and desires are limited by a financial payment. The borrower is truly in bondage to the lender. You have to pay your payment. If that is not bad enough, many students who have a large student loan debt are staring bankruptcy straight in the face.

If you currently have college loans, commit to paying for the rest of your schooling without any more loans. You will need an action plan to get rid of this debt faster than simply paying the minimum payment. You might need a higher paying job or a commitment to a less luxurious lifestyle so you can be freed from the financial bondage of student loan debt.

When you look at the numbers that show how much you pay on loans over a lifetime, it is so much more than you would have anticipated. When you get a loan for $60,000, you usually do not take into consideration the amount of interest you will have to pay, not to mention your monthly payment. But the numbers speak for themselves. Look at the following example:

Loan Balance:	$60,000
Adjusted Loan Balance:	$60,000
Loan Interest Rate:	6.80%
Loan Fees:	0.00%
Loan Term:	10 years
Monthly Loan Payment:	**$690.48**
Number of Payments:	120
Cumulative Payments:	$82,857.94
Total Interest Paid:	$22,857.94

(http://www.finaid.org/calculators/scripts/loanpayments.cgi)

Your monthly payment on a $60,000 student loan would be $690.48 per month at an interest rate of 6.8%. But, by paying for college as you go, you can save over $22,000!

The bottom line is that student loans put you in debt. Most students don't think about it. But by reading this, you have just been blessed. You have found the pot of gold at the end of the rainbow. The pot of gold is this: you can avoid debt. Although many people get loans for college, there are people who go through college and graduate without any debt. I was one of those people. You can be one too!

I have no student loans to pay back. Do you know how big of a relief that is? It's hard to imagine until you are on the other side. Just wait until you graduate and you will feel the relief too. There is just something about waking up in the morning and not having to pay a $600 to $800 student loan bill every month. It makes the sun shine brighter!

Remember, too, that loans are not meant to finance your living expenses. Get a job if you can't afford your life.

If you are not going to pay for your school on student loans, you will need a plan of how you will pay for school. Scholarships are a great place to start. Schools offer a variety of scholarships, including academic, athletic, and private scholarships. There are also many grants available. We will talk about some of these options later in the next chapter.

COLLEGE IN REAL LIFE

SUMMARY:

- A secret to succeeding in college is being responsible with your money.

- A budget will help you monitor bills, expenses, and your income.

- Credit cards and debt are not the answer. Work to pay for college.

RESOURCES:

- SavingAdvice.com

- MoneyInstructor.com

MAKE IT PRACTICAL:

1. Write down the amount of your income.

2. In a separate column, write down your expenses.

3. Subtract your expenses from your income.

4. Follow the **3N Budget Method.**

5. You are on your way to having a personal budget!

References:
[1] Mint, www.mint.com ©2010 Intuit, Inc.

CHAPTER EIGHT

Scholarships, Grants, and Other Ways to Pay for College

"One secret of success in life is for a man to be ready for his opportunity when it comes."
– Benjamin Disraeli

When you start your first semester, you will go through financial registration. This is where you work out the financial details of school. Basically, you are letting the school know how you are going to pay for your education. If you are making monthly payments, you will have to sign a promissory note, which is a document that states that you will pay your bill. You have to be at least 18 years old to sign it. If you graduated high school early and are younger than 18, make sure you have a parent with you. They will have to sign the promissory note as well, since you would be considered a minor.

I was unaware of the promissory note when I went to financial registration for the first time. Since I was only 17, I couldn't sign it myself, complicating the issue and making hundreds of students wait longer in the line. Let's just say the glances and glares were enough to confirm my unpopular status that day. However, I was able to arrange for an exception and bring the promissory note back later that day. The pride of being my own person was slowly going down the drain. But I learned that even when you go to college, you still need people to help you, parents included.

Financial registration can seem stressful, especially if you are not good with numbers. Take it one step at a time and ask questions as needed.

FREE MONEY

What if someone told you that you could go to college for free? You would probably fall out of your chair. How can you go to college for free? Scholarships.

SMART TALK

Based on academic performance, merit, or need, scholarships pay your school tuition. You will have to be assertive in finding out what scholarships are available, their deadlines, and the process of applying for them. **The people who apply for scholarships are the people who get them.**

Based on academic performance, merit, or need, scholarships pay your school tuition. New scholarships are available every semester and every year. However, they will not come knocking on your door, begging you to apply. You will have to be assertive in finding out what scholarships are available, their deadlines, and the process of applying for them. The people who apply for scholarships are the people who get them. If you don't apply for a scholarship, you won't get one.

Getting scholarships is probably the area that requires the most assertiveness. Why? Because everyone wants one. On the other hand, don't disqualify yourself from receiving a scholarship by not applying. Scholarships frequently come available because the current scholarship recipient is graduating, transferring schools, or did not maintain the designated requirements. Stay up-to-date on scholarship offerings and keep pursuing scholarships even if you are not awarded one at first.

Are academics important for getting a scholarship? Yes. Although you might get an athletic scholarship to college, which is awarded based on your athletic abilities rather than your academic achievements, you will have to take classes in college and will have to maintain a certain GPA in order to keep receiving the scholarship. Therefore, academics are always important.

Some schools do offer "full-ride" scholarships, meaning everything is paid for by the scholarship. But the ratio of full-ride scholarships to the number of students is usually low. However, don't become discouraged. You can have multiple scholarships at lesser amounts; the numbers add up quickly. Free money via scholarships always counts!

So if tuition costs $4,000 per semester and you get two scholarships for $1,000 each per semester, you will have to pay $2,000 each semester for tuition. You would then need to figure how much that would be per month, hence your school bill. Start pinching your pennies. Although it might seem like a lot at the time, it will be worth paying it up front in the long run! Are you catching on to the theme? School debt can be avoided.

How do you get scholarships? Apply for them, and, while you are at it, apply for every scholarship that is somewhat applicable to you. Some state schools have a "bright flight" program for students who earn a certain score on their ACT. If you are within a point or two of the score requirement, you can take the ACT again to try to score higher. This "bright flight" program offers part or full scholarships to students.

WORK FOR YOUR MONEY

Okay, so you have decided you are going to pay for school as you go. You have a job and maybe a small scholarship. But you need more money, so you decide you need more work. Fortunately, there are ways to make money that are temporary or seasonal.

> **SMART TALK**
>
> **Don't overlook any opportunities for work.** It might be the answer to your money problems.

Around the holidays, many retailers hire people for a temporary amount of time, and this is a great way to make some extra money. Also, people need yards mowed, houses cleaned, tutors for high school students, and babysitters for children. Although these things might seem menial and out of your league because you are now in college, don't overlook any opportunities for work. It might be the answer to your money problems.

Schools often have job/career centers where you can find information about current temporary jobs. Don't let your pride stand in the way. Getting a professor or past employer to refer you will also help you in finding additional work. Working and paying for school as you go will benefit you in the future. You will be able to look at your hard work with pride and have great satisfaction.

GRANTS

You can also apply for grants. Grants are different from student loans, as grants are based on financial need...and you usually don't have to pay them back. Most grants come from the government, whereas scholarships come from institutions, companies, or the private sector. Some grants have requirements that are attached to them, such as maintaining a certain financial or academic status.

To be able to apply for a grant, you will need to have filled out your Free Application for Federal Student Aid (FAFSA) form. Since most grants are government based, you have to do your fair share of paperwork. The most common government grant is the Pell Grant. Applications for the Pell Grant are based on a combination of expected family contribution, tuition rates, and full-time enrollment. The Pell Grant is just one example of a federal program that is available for students with financial need.

ONLINE CLASSES

Online classes can be financially beneficial, and they are increasing in popularity. Taking some classes online allows you greater flexibility in your schedule, which means you really can have a job that fits your college schedule. However, don't be misled that online courses are easy. Since you will not be in the classroom, you will "make up" that time in studying, tests, and papers.

To do online classes, you need to be self-motivated. Your success will depend on your personal work ethic more than a regular class. So it's a trade-off. By having a more flexible schedule, you forfeit the personal interaction with your classmates and professor, as well as in-class learning time.

FAST TRACK TIP

Taking some classes online allows you greater flexibility in your schedule, which means you really can have a job that fits your college schedule. **Your success will depend on your personal work ethic** more than a regular class.

From personal experience, online classes can be a challenge. They are not impossible, just a challenge. You have less structure and it can be more difficult to contact your professor. However, in my case, the certain class fit my schedule and enabled me to do class on my own time; hence, the trade-off.

If you don't stay on top of your online class, you will let everything pile up until the last week of the semester, making it impossible for you to get it done. If you are unsure about online classes, take one and see how it goes. Then, make your decision about online classes based on how well you did in that class.

I knew someone who took a semester of online classes at a community college. Everything was going fine until the last month of class when he admitted he had not done any of the work yet. Unfortunately, he was unable to complete all the classes he was enrolled in. While he was busy with life and working, his online classes were building up the workload over the semester. His procrastination cost him time and money.

If you are going to do online school, you need to set yourself up for success. Do you have the time to commit to the number of classes you are taking? Are you motivated to do them without any outside guidance or motivation? Online classes can be a great way to take classes around a busy work schedule; just be prepared to get motivated!

CREATE YOUR FINANCIAL LEGACY

As you can see, you have many options for funding your college education. You can go to college without getting students loans! To do so, you will need a plan, initiative, and a good work ethic. I challenge you to do all you can to avoid student loans. Pursue all other options. Some students who pay for school as they go take off a semester to save money so they can pay for the rest of college. But between CLEP tests, online classes, and summer school, you can quickly make up that lost time and even come out ahead.

Whenever I think about student loans, I think about my dad and his college experience. When I was growing up he often told me how he made every tuition payment, and when he walked out the doors after graduation, the college bill was paid. Although it came with sacrifices, the example he gave me was priceless.

You are living a legacy that you will pass on. It is hard to imagine that when you are 18, 19, or 20, but it is true. The wisdom about school debt was passed on to me, which I will pass on to my children. Now, that's a legacy!

COLLEGE IN REAL LIFE

SUMMARY:

- In a culture where everyone wants to fit in, stand out by not getting student loans and finding alternative ways to pay for school.

- Scholarships help you go to college free!

- Grants are based on financial need.

RESOURCES:

- Fastweb.com enables you to search for scholarships.

- Scholarships.com provides information about scholarships.

- GoCollege.com provides information about grants.

MAKE IT PRACTICAL:

1. Research the scholarships your school offers.

2. Fill out the application for the scholarship and submit it.

3. Repeat step two multiple times.

4. Ask students about scholarships that might not be advertised.

CHAPTER NINE
How to Deal with the "Stuff" that Happens

"Impossible is just a big word thrown around by small men who find it easier to live in the world they've been given than to explore the power they have to change it. Impossible is not a fact. It's an opinion. Impossible is not a declaration. It's a dare. Impossible is potential. Impossible is temporary. Impossible is nothing."
– Muhammad Ali

Stress is a part of everyone's life. There's no escaping it. What's important is how you handle it. Those students who handle stress well and take steps to minimize it tend to do better in school and in life—even if they're on the fast track and trying to graduate college early.

If your life has been smooth sailing all through high school, you may find the realities of college to be a bit stressful. Don't worry—you can handle anything that comes your way. You just have to know what to expect.

CREATE BALANCE

Most students have to work while they are going to school. Whether you work part-time or full-time, you really can balance both work and school so you don't get overwhelmed or stressed.

First, if you don't have a job but need one, don't be picky. Find a place that is hiring and apply—it really doesn't matter what type of company it is or the type of job. You are better off getting a job now—any job—rather than waiting for the perfect opportunity to knock on your door.

Before you accept a job offer, make sure your work and school schedules don't conflict. If they do, make arrangements with work or with school to accommodate the other. If you must work full-time while going to school, remember that most schools have night classes, online classes, or degree completion programs. Since working full-time would be the exception for most college students, I will focus on students working part-time.

FAST TRACK TIP

We all need to learn the art of balancing our lives and schedules, especially when you're trying to compress your college years.

So, how do you juggle work and school? If you have ever watched an inexperienced juggler, you've seen that they usually drop a ball very quickly. And as soon as one ball drops, the rest come tumbling down as well.

The same concept applies to juggling your life. When you try to juggle work, school, homework, family, and friends, you usually drop a ball somewhere. Then, everything suffers. Since no one is a superman or wonder woman, we all need to learn the art of balancing our lives and schedules, especially when you're trying to compress your college years.

When something is balanced, the sum of all the parts equals the whole. Therefore, the combination of work, school, homework, family, and friends has to equal one life—your life. You only have a certain amount of time in each day, just like everyone else. Why, then, do some people seem like they have more time to fit everything in, while others barely sleep at night before it's time to wake-up and do it all over again?

The answer has more to do with time management than anything else. Time management is simply being able to manage your time well. At the core of time management is self-management—the ability to manage your life and time in such a way that you are productive.

Time is a valuable commodity that you cannot regain once it's lost. That's why you need to make good decisions regarding the way you use your time. You cannot be two places at the same time, so you need to invest your time into productive activities.

> ## SMART TALK
>
> You have limited time; you can't do everything every week. However, if you manage your time well, **you will be able to do the important things and some fun things, too.**

The best way to keep track of your time is to create a detailed schedule for yourself. In your schedule, some things such as work, school, and homework are mandatory—they have to be part of your weekly schedule and time management plan no matter what. Other things, however, such as going shopping, playing video games, and even hanging out with friends, are negotiable items — they can appear in your schedule only when time allows.

To plan your weekly schedule, first fill in all the absolutes, such as class times and work schedule. Then, fill in the gaps in your schedule with extra meetings you may have, as well as study time, family events, time with friends, etc. Remember that you have limited time; you can't do everything every week. However, if you manage your time well, you will be able to do the important things and some fun things, too. Try out your schedule for a couple of weeks; then make any changes as needed.

The largest challenge to effective time management is time wasters, which are unproductive activities that last multiple hours. Common time wasters are video games, partying, or watching television. If there is not enough room in your schedule for everything, you will have to let a negotiable item go. Also, if you are forced to choose between two extracurricular activities, pick the activity you like the most and let the other one go. Although it might seem like a hard decision at the time, it will keep you from being stretched too thin.

DON'T STRESS

You might still be wondering if it's possible to really balance it all. Yes, it is. Just make sure you don't allow your schedule to overwhelm you. When you are overwhelmed, you can lose perspective and

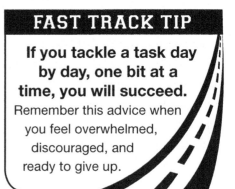

FAST TRACK TIP

If you tackle a task day by day, one bit at a time, you will succeed. Remember this advice when you feel overwhelmed, discouraged, and ready to give up.

become emotional. Everything can feel like it is caving in on you, causing you to want to give up. That's when life becomes emotional and you feel as though you are on a roller coaster.

For example, every semester when I went to the first class and received my syllabus, I'd look at all the homework, projects, tests, and quizzes and immediately feel overwhelmed. How was I ever going to get it all done? Well, how do you eat a whole elephant? The answer: One bite at a time. Likewise, how do you graduate from college? By taking college one day at a time. You won't get everything done on day one. But if you tackle it day by day, one bit at a time, you will succeed. Remember this advice whenever you feel overwhelmed and discouraged.

Now that you're in college, you need to learn how to manage stress. Stress comes in all shapes and sizes. The pressures of school, the financial demands, and impending deadlines create stress. Realize, though, that stress is not always a bad thing, as it helps you get things done and become motivated. However, if you do not control stress, it will control you.

When you allow stress to build up, it becomes unmanageable. The solution? Deal with it before you become completely overwhelmed.

Here's a simple process for how to do that.

- First, when you become stressed, admit it. Realizing you are stressed is vital to overcoming the stress.

- Then, identify the item or items that are causing the stress. Why is

SMART TALK

The way you deal with stress in college will form a habit for how you deal with stress **for the rest of your life.**

it making you stressed? For example, do you not have enough time to create the project?

- Next, problem-solve to minimize or eliminate the stress. If you don't have enough time to finish a project, how can you rearrange your schedule to create more time for the project? Maybe you need to find someone who can cover your shift at work or cancel a meeting or decline going out with friends.

- After you problem-solve, act on one of the options to reduce some of the stress.

Learning to deal with stress is a life-long discipline. There will always be things that cause you stress. The way you deal with stress in college will form a habit for how you will deal with stress for the rest of your life.

AVOID PROCRASTINATION

When fun comes knocking at your door, is your first inclination to decline and ask your friends to reschedule in a couple of weeks when you are less busy? No, the excitement of doing something at the spur of the moment is so exhilarating that you often have a momentary lapse of logical thinking and throw your books on the ground to go join in, even though your test is only 14 hours and 43 minutes away. Hanging out with friends really is fun. But as the clock keeps ticking, you just can't stop thinking about that test tomorrow, which is really stealing all the fun from being spontaneous.

Doing things you enjoy is not the enemy of success. What a relief! But the trade-off leads to procrastination, which, in full bloom, will sabotage your efforts to be on the dean's list, to get scholarships, to graduate early, and maybe even to continue on to graduate school. If your famous last words are "I will do it later," you can rest assured that there

FAST TRACK TIP

Procrastination, when in full bloom, will sabotage your efforts to graduate early. **To succeed in college, you must kiss procrastination good-bye.**

is hope. You can succeed in college and kiss procrastination good-bye for good. Here are a few success tips to keep in mind:

- Schedule something "fun" into your week, even if your week is booked with tests and studying.

- Stop justifying spending your time on the computer or texting. It's not helping you get anything done.

- Turn your phone on silent and unplug the computer for a designated amount of focused studying time.

- Reward yourself after you finish your task rather than before. If you want to be on the computer, reward yourself with time on the computer or hanging out with friends after you study.

When you stop procrastinating, the feeling of being overwhelmed will go away, and your stress will diminish. Procrastination really is the enemy of academic success. Don't let it control your destiny!

JUST SAY "NO"

Although "no" is one of the first words we learn as children, our ability to use it in our daily vocabulary decreases as we get older. Everyone wants a piece of you...yes, you! They want your time, energy, resourc-

FAST TRACK TIP

You simply can't do everything for everyone all the time. Therefore, choose groups or extracurricular activities that are important to you, and say "no" to all the others.

es, expertise, experience, humor, house, etc. Although they might have good intentions or their request might be for a good cause, everyone will try to consume your life. They will want you to be involved in all the school groups, activities, events, and committees. It's common for people to get lost in the energy of popularity.

But you simply can't do everything for everyone all the time. It's not possible. Therefore, it's important you choose groups or extracurricular activities that are important to you. Then, practice saying "no" to all the others.

Everyone together now... "no." Say it out loud. "No." You are going to have to learn the art of saying "no" to the unimportant so you can say "yes" to the things you really want to do. It is all about prioritization. You must have your priorities straight to have balance in your life.

PUT FEAR IN ITS PLACE

We all experience uncertainty at times and become afraid. When you are dealing with fear, talk with someone. If you don't deal with fear, it can become a life-controlling issue.

SMART TALK

FEAR is an acronym for False Evidence Appearing Real. In other words, many times your fears are unfounded and you CAN do something to change the situation.

What are you afraid of? Are you experiencing fear because of your classes, where you live, or health problems? You do not have to be afraid. By talking with someone, you can determine if your fear is legitimate. As the old saying goes, FEAR is an acronym for False Evidence Appearing Real. In other words, many times your fears are unfounded and you CAN do something to change the situation.

For example, if you are afraid of change, choose to turn your fear into excitement. If you are afraid you are making the wrong decision, you'll often find that the fear dissipates when you just make a decision and stick with it.

Fear does not have to control you. Ask for help. Being afraid of college is not going to move you in the direction of your goals. Just shift your perspective from fear and uncertainty to excitement and anticipation. Your environment and situation don't necessarily have to change—sometimes a change in perspective is all you need. For example, just because you're alone doesn't mean you have to be lonely. It's just a shift in perspective.

You will be encountering many things that could be intimidating. New friends. New school. New challenges. Change your perspective to see the opportunity that is surrounding you. New opportunities lie before you as you enter a new season of life. Embrace the change, as change is the only way to move forward.

MEDICAL EMERGENCIES

We all get sick. When you are living in a dorm with a bunch of people, germs tend to get passed around. That's why you have to take care of yourself to minimize sickness. Make sure you wash your hands and clean your room for prevention.

When you do get sick, go see the school nurse. Most schools have a wellness office with a medical professional who can help you when you are sick. If you miss more than two days of class because you are too sick to get out of bed, go get help.

If your roommate is sick, you can do a few things to minimize the spread of germs. Wash your hands religiously. Make sure that your roommate stays confined to a certain space. Disinfect your room and doorknobs twice a day. Spend limited time with your roommate until he or she is better. Eat plenty of fruits and vegetables, and drink water to keep your immune system strong. Eating junk food will not help you stay well.

What do you do when you are faced with an **emergency?** A friend of mine was dealing with ongoing fainting and other symptoms. One night, I had to pick her up from work because she had fainted. Another night, it became an emergency because she was having trouble walking. I took her to the emergency room.

When you are facing an emergency, stay calm and contact people who can help you. Whether it is taking someone to the emergency room or telling an authority, you won't have to carry the burden alone.

SMART TALK

When you are facing an emergency, **stay calm and contact people who can help you.** Whether it is taking someone to the emergency room or telling an authority, you won't have to carry the burden alone.

Fortunately, everything turned out all right for my friend, but it was a long night.

You never know when people around you might be in need. Whether a roommate is struggling with depression or a friend needs to go to the emergency room, knowing whom to contact is important. Having emergency numbers can help you take care of situations outside of your control. If someone is in a life-threatening situation, someone who can help needs to know. On the other hand, if that someone who needs help is you, let someone know. There are people in the counseling and wellness centers at colleges who want to help you.

No matter what you face during college, from time stealers to internal fears, know that you can overcome it. Nothing is impossible when you surround yourself with support and believe in your goals.

COLLEGE IN REAL LIFE

SUMMARY:

- One of the best ways to minimize stress is to avoid procrastination.

- Effectively managing your time will increase your productivity and success.

- Procrastination is the enemy of academic success.

MAKE IT PRACTICAL:

1. When you are assigned a project, work on it that week.

2. Divide the project into weekly segments until the due date.

3. Have the project ready at least one day before the due date.

CHAPTER TEN
Graduation Day

*"I shall be telling this with a sigh somewhere ages
and ages hence: Two roads diverged in a wood, and I –
I took the one less traveled by, and that has
made all the difference."*
– Robert Frost

before you know it, graduation day will arrive. Your family and friends will be abuzz as the ceremony draws near. Lining up with your peers wearing long black robes and squares hats will make even the hardest heart flutter with excitement. Professors will be shuffling through the lobby in their academic attire. You'll be ready to go. Dream about it now. It will be a reality very soon.

FAST TRACK TIP

When you start college and throughout your entire college experience, always envision yourself graduating. **Although graduation seems forever away, it will be here before you know it.**

On your big day, take time to smile and revel in your accomplishment. No matter what anyone said you could or couldn't do, smile because the knowledge, experiences, and disciplines you learned will have changed who you are, for the better.

When you start college and throughout your entire college experience, always envision yourself graduating. Although graduation seems forever away, it will be here before you know it. College goes by quickly. Keep graduating from college as a goal in the forefront of your mind. Let it motivate you when you feel tired and burnt out. There will be moments when you want to quit. You will see friends who are out of school, and on the surface it might seem easier to just give up on school. No matter what, keep going, even when it would seem easier to quit. Your time in college is short in comparison to your whole life. Enjoy the time you have to study, grow, and develop.

As you approach graduation, the moment will feel surreal. You will have imagined that moment for years. You will have put time, energy, sweat, and tears into your college education, and it will be finally coming to a close. The infamous "senioritis" will have commenced, and you will feel ready to take on the world. You will feel more than ready to exchange all of the preparation for a black robe, hat, and diploma. A college graduation is a rite of passage worth acknowledgement. You have arrived at a milestone in your life. It is worth celebrating!

THE POMP AND CIRCUMSTANCE

The graduation ceremony is part of the celebration. Go to your graduation ceremony! The finality of the accomplishment will not resonate in you unless you go. A graduation ceremony simply honors students' hard work and determination to finish. Be a person who finishes, no matter how long it takes. Even if you are a non-traditional student in the midst of

SMART TALK

Go to your graduation ceremony! The finality of the accomplishment will not resonate in you unless you go.

younger peers, celebrate your accomplishment. It is a significant moment in your life. You will be able to look back at that moment for years to come with pride.

Your name will be announced over the loud speakers as everyone cheers. Make sure the announcer knows how to pronounce your name. At my Baccalaureate rehearsal, my first, middle, and last name were all pronounced incorrectly. My friends around me giggled, and on the way back to my seat, I received more than a couple "I'm sorry." I just smiled, but after the rehearsal was over, I walked up to the front and spoke with the professor announcing the graduates. After thorough review, I hoped for better at my actual graduation.

Before I was being announced at the real graduation, I quickly pronounced my name for him as I handed him my name on paper. I held my breath and started walking across the stage. He said my name correctly, and I smiled. I was finally graduating.

If you have a complicated name, speak to the professor stating names prior to graduation. You will want your name pronounced as correctly as possible. Even if it goes terribly wrong, smile and keep walking. The people who count will know who you are.

TIMING IS EVERYTHING

Some people graduate in May and others graduate in December. If you are on the traditional four-year plan, then you should graduate in May. However, if you are graduating early, it is likely that you would graduate in the summer or December.

When I graduated from college, it was in December. Because of the size of my school, they only had one graduation ceremony each year. It would have been so easy for me to miss it. After all, I was out of college for five months now. Even so, I attended my graduation. I walked the stage in my black robe and was handed a diploma that marked a moment in my life. Looking back, I am so glad I went. There is something about being surrounded by graduating peers and professors in their academic attire that is exciting.

When I was in graduate school, I had a friend who was graduating from college, and she wasn't going to go to her graduation. She didn't have any family that would be there, and to her, it didn't seem to matter. We talked about it, and after much debate she decided to go. She didn't regret it. So if you are unsure in your decision, decide to go to your graduation. You won't regret it.

EVERY GOOD THING MUST COME TO AN END

For some people, graduation is bittersweet. It's the end of one chapter in life. But while you are leaving behind friends and memories, you are embarking on the next journey of your life.

Confronting your emotions about graduation is important. Some people want to stay in college forever. I am not going to lie; college is fun. It is a time to grow and become the person you were meant to be. But our lives are not meant to be confined to one season of life. You have to realize that there is more for you. College has just been part of the process.

SMART TALK

Life didn't abruptly "begin" when you started college, and it doesn't "begin" after college. If you have the notion that life begins after college, you will become disappointed that everything doesn't automatically change and go as originally planned.

For others, graduation is it—the day you have been waiting for your whole life. It is exciting, but there is no magic fairy dust where all your dreams instantly come true. Life didn't abruptly "begin" when you started college, and it doesn't "begin" after college. You are currently living your life. What you do with it makes a difference. If you have the notion that life begins after college, you will become disappointed that everything doesn't automatically change and go as originally planned. There are always going to be bumps along the way. Life is a journey. Enjoy the ride.

Getting to graduation day takes determination, perseverance, and resilience. You need determination to keep going when things get hard, perseverance to keep studying when you get tired, and resilience to press on when you fail. Graduation is the culmination of all these characteristics. Be determined, and it will pay off. Happy Graduation!

COLLEGE IN REAL LIFE

SUMMARY:

- When you start college, envision yourself graduating.

- Life didn't abruptly "begin" when you started college, and it doesn't "begin" after college. You are currently living your life. What you do with it makes a difference.

- Life is a journey. Enjoy the ride.

MAKE IT PRACTICAL:

1. Be prepared your last year to graduate by filling out the correct graduation papers.

2. Order your cap and gown.

3. Smile when you graduate.

CHAPTER ELEVEN
Life After College

"It was a high counsel that I once heard given to a young person,
'Always do what you are afraid to do.'"
– Ralph Waldo Emerson

"Can I leave yet?"

My friend smiled and shook his head, "No."

College wasn't even over yet but I knew one thing for sure: I was never going to grad school. Then again, "never" has a way of signing us up for the unexpected. As the saying goes, "Never say never."

Toward the end of your senior year of college, you will be on the job hunt or making decisions about graduate school. Graduate school is not for everyone but is increasingly becoming a job requirement. Some people choose to go to graduate school right after college, while others wait a few years. Depending on your field, a graduate degree may or may not be beneficial.

GRADUATE SCHOOL

During your senior year of college, you will encounter recruiters from different schools who come to promote graduate school. They came to some of my classes to talk about different programs at their schools. I would always quietly sigh and ask my neighbor if I could leave yet. I had absolutely no plans of going to school any longer. I just didn't think it was for me.

SMART TALK

Graduate school is not for everyone but is increasingly becoming a job requirement. Some people choose to go to graduate school right after college, while others wait a few years. **Depending on your field, a graduate degree may or may not be beneficial.**

I graduated in December from college with my bachelor's degree, and by the following May, my dad started talking to me about grad school as a possibility. To be honest, I wasn't interested. But by mid-June, when I was helping at a youth camp, I began to feel like I should go to grad school. As I began to process my future, I realized that I would be positively positioning myself by continuing my education. I couldn't believe it; I had a change of heart.

When I got home from the camp, I applied for an MBA program and received an acceptance letter within a couple of weeks. Acceptance was contingent on my GMAT score, which I had yet to take. Considering that the application deadline was only a couple of weeks away when I applied, I was fortunate. After I applied to the school, I took the GMAT.

Again, graduate school isn't for everyone, but if you are considering it at all, explore your options thoroughly. Your options will depend upon your field of study and application requirements. The process of deciding, applying, and going to grad school are all similar to going to college. Make sure your decision fits your goals and dreams for your life. Then, you won't have to live with regret either way. For me, when it came down to it, I knew I would regret not continuing my education. I don't want to live with regret, and neither do you!

To get into grad school, you will have to take a standardized entrance exam. The most common one is the GRE, which stands for Graduate Record Exam. However, most law schools and business schools require the LSAT and GMAT respectively, while medical schools require the MCAT. That's a lot of abbreviations! Check to see which test is applicable to the school you are applying.

You can buy resource books for each test at bookstores or online. From my personal experience of taking the GMAT, you have to study. It is important that you do well. These tests are not usually of-

FAST TRACK TIP

When you go to graduate school, make sure you **know the reason you are going.** It's an investment of time, money, and energy that you don't want to use without a plan.

fered at a school but rather at a testing facility. They cost a couple hundred dollars, so you want to be serious about taking it. It's not a test you can just take whenever you want because of the time and cost involved.

Some graduate programs are more competitive than others, having higher acceptance standards. Researching schools and programs is all part of the process. See what the entrance exam score requirements are at your prospective graduate schools. After you take the test, you will have a better idea of what requirements you meet when applying at different schools.

You will also have to submit a graduate admissions essay. You will need to include your intentions, goals, and reasons to be accepted in an essay format. Each school has different guidelines. Some schools will require a sample essay on a specified topic to determine your writing, critical thinking, and analytical skills. Writing admissions essays takes time. Hence, deciding early about grad school can give you time to adequately prepare.

Finally, when you go to grad school, make sure you know the reason you are going. It is an investment of time, money, and energy that you don't want to use without a plan. The classes will be more challenging and demanding, requiring you to be committed to your decision.

NEW DIRECTIONS

What happens if you go to college, graduate, and hate your career/job? Is there an answer for a career mistake? If you went through your undergrad years and now want to switch fields, you can get your masters in a different field. (I just stopped tears for some of you, didn't I?)

No, you do not have to be a history teacher for the rest of your life if you hate it. But let's make a better decision this next go around. How about it? Although your simplest path to grad school would be in a similar field, you can branch out. There will be prerequisites you will have to do before you are ac-

FAST TRACK TIP

If you want a career change, write down a plan—a plan is going to help you decide between your options. Since you don't want to spend your whole life in school, **having a written plan will help you avoid being in school for years.**

cepted into the actual program. Depending on the switch, it might just take a semester of additional courses to prepare you for the graduate program for which you are applying.

Another option is to complete a certificate program that would enable you to do something different than your current job. Certificate programs are more like training in a specific area instead of a degree. They take less time and could be helpful in getting a promotion or job switch.

If you want a career change, write down a plan—a plan is going to help you decide between your options. Write down the pros and cons of changing careers. If possible, getting a graduate degree that is complementary to your undergraduate degree could help position you more competitively in the workplace.

Since you don't want to spend your whole life in school, having a written plan will help you avoid being in school for years. If you are confused about your decision, moving forward will bring clarity. Deciding to change careers is a significant decision. If you're not sure your decision is right, just do something, anything. Failing to move forward will negatively affect your mental state. Don't allow yourself to go there.

Move forward in your education or career. Sitting idle will not create more opportunities for you.

GET REAL

Let me tell you something...getting a Master's degree does not come with magic fairy dust either. You get out of a program what you put into it, and the worth of your degree depends on what you do with it. A master's degree does not guarantee you a job. But, if you are applying for a job with a master's degree versus others with their bachelor's degree, you have a chance at standing out in the crowd. A master's degree expands your learning, increases your critical thinking skills, and provides a more concentrated learning experience on a specific subject.

> ## SMART TALK
>
> A master's degree does not guarantee you a job. But, if you are applying for a job with a master's degree versus others with their bachelor's degree, **you have a chance at standing out in the crowd.**

Many people go to graduate school; fewer students graduate. When I started, many people thought I would not finish—not because my work ethic had indicated that, but because few people actually see it to completion. A lot of people start, but starting is only half the battle. If you are going to go to grad school, go all the way and finish your degree.

Graduating with my master's degree was a very exciting day. It had seemed so impossible in my mind when I started.

I had heard horror stories and met people who had been in the program almost five years. But, class-by-class, semester-by-semester, I was closer to the finish line. When I sat in the graduation ceremony, I got a text about what someone said about me. They said, "She just didn't quit." That might be more profound than I gave them credit for. Nonetheless, it is a huge compliment.

What are people who are watching your life saying about you? Can they say that you just don't quit? Graduating and completing something requires a "no quitting" attitude. By choosing not to quit you are setting yourself up to succeed in life. You will always face situations where you are tempted to quit. Persevering even when it's hard is a discipline you will carry with you throughout your life. If you put your mind to it, you can complete grad school!

FINDING A JOB

If you choose to enter the workforce rather than go to grad school, apply for jobs before you graduate. You will be glad you did. Being prepared usually decreases worry, anxiety, and uncertainty.

SMART TALK

If you choose to enter the workforce rather than go to grad school, **apply for jobs *before* you graduate.** You will be glad you did.

Applying for a job will require you to have a résumé and cover letter or letter of intent. The cover letter details the job for which you are applying and highlights your work, educational experience, and community involvement. The cover letter should always end with a call to action. You can give information on how the employer can contact you or state when you are going to follow-up.

The résumé should have detailed work, education, and volunteer information. It should highlight job skills and interpersonal skills. Although a résumé can be personal, it still needs to be professional. Use verbs that describe your current role at your job or past jobs. Don't embellish your résumé with false information. However, structure it so that your strengths are prominent. Creating a quality résumé and cover letter will take time and effort. But it's worth it. A professional, eye-catching résumé can help you get a foot in the door and possibly an interview.

When you go to a job interview, the way you dress is important. You would be better off to be overdressed in a suit and tie rather than show up to an interview in jeans and a t-shirt. Whether you dress business professional or business casual depends upon the type of business you are entering. However, showing up to an interview with a suit and tie will always make a positive impression. Business casual would be dress pants and a collared shirt. Although business casual might be dressy for you, opt to take your appearance to the next level for a job interview. These simple steps will help you in your search for a job.

SUMMARY:

- Graduate school is not for everyone but it is increasingly becoming a job requirement.

- If you want to go to graduate school to change careers, write down a plan.

- If you choose to enter the workforce rather than go to grad school, apply for jobs before you graduate.

RESOURCES:

- GradSchools.com

- Visit individual school websites.

MAKE IT PRACTICAL:

1. Research and pick your top three grad school choices.

2. Apply to all three schools.

3. Evaluate based on acceptance.

CONCLUSION
Write Your Own Story

*"If you can imagine it, you can achieve it; if you can
dream it, you can become it."*
– William Arthur Ward

many components have to come together when you go to college. Being aware and prepared can be half the battle. The second half of the battle is persevering until the end. As you discover yourself and pursue your passion, remember the people in your life. You will need family and friends through the process of college and beyond. People are important. Your family and friends make the exciting times more exciting and the sad times less sad. Make them a priority in your life.

Since you are driving down the sunny road to college and beyond, enjoy the journey. Life is about the journey more than the destination. Make time to smell the roses along the way. Stop and pick a few flowers, and relish the present moment. College goes by quickly. No matter what speed your speedometer is set on, make the most of it. Even if the college road is speedy for you, embrace it and live with no regrets.

Although I graduated from college in two and half years, the experience was great. If I could do it all over again, I would—not because I have regrets, but because I grew more into the person I am today. When I think of college, my mind starts racing with the stories I have shared with you, the people I met, the friendships I made, and the discipline I learned. It all collides into a beautiful picture titled "college" in my mind.

Always remember that you are a winner and you can succeed. In fact, put this on your bathroom mirror and repeat it to yourself every day: "I am a winner. I will succeed. I am a winner. I will succeed...."

There is power in our words and thoughts that can help us fulfill our destiny. Believe in yourself regardless of other's opinions. I believe there is a reason you picked up this book—no matter who you are or where you are going, embrace the purpose for your life. College is an amazing opportunity to learn and grow. It will propel you forward into your destiny by preparing and equipping you. Even when it seems like just another ordinary day, remember that life is comprised of ordinary days all squished together. Take your ordinary day and make something of it.

Wherever you are on the college journey, I hope you are filled with a sigh of relief. I hope that some of the weight of uncertainty has been lifted off your shoulders. After reading this book, you should feel a little more prepared for college and know what to expect. The gray areas of college should be fading away into firm shades of black and white.

As you enter this new season of life, you will have questions. When you have questions, feel free to use this book as a reference...and ask those around you for help. There's no shame in asking for help.

College is a time of preparation. You are building your life. Keep dreaming. Strive to fulfill your goals day-by-day. But, when all is said and done, may someone say this of you: "You just never gave up."

You have your whole life to live. It's time to live it!

APPENDIX

COLLEGE ROOKIE GUIDELINES FOR SUCCESS

Here are some quick tips to help you make the most of your college years.

1. SLEEP

Rest is important in all functions of life. When you start losing substantial amounts of sleep, your physical health is not the only thing in danger. Your mental and emotional well-being depend on rest. Sleep has to be a priority, even when everyone else is staying up all night to "study." If you want to succeed, stop trying to be like everyone else. Set your own rhythm and follow it.

When I moved on campus my second year of college, the challenge was that everyone stayed up late. During my first week, some people wanted to go out to eat at 11 p.m. I agreed. By the time I arrived back in my room, I was so exhausted, but I had class at 8 a.m. the next morning. Luckily, it was the first week of the semester, and I learned my lesson.

Sleep helps us to have perspective. When we are well rested, we make better decisions and can cope with stress. My mother always told me that no day was too bad that a nap couldn't fix it. I think she was on to something. When we get good rest, we don't respond to life in a panic and can think clearly. However, the opposite is also true. When we don't get enough sleep, we are cranky, not fully present, and are distracted by our tiredness or mood. When everyone is vying for your time, don't let sleep get placed at the bottom of the list.

2. PERSONAL DEVELOPMENT

College is a great time for personal development. You are experiencing some freedom for the first time. You can be whoever you want to be. You will have many new experiences, and it is important that you stand by your values through it all.

Character seems harder and harder to come by. With so many business people involved in fraud, it seems that character has no value in the workplace. In reality, companies are looking for well-grounded people who can stand up for their beliefs. The truth is more expensive than a lie, but a lie costs you more than truth does. Did you get that? You might need to read it again. The truth is like buying a pair of leather shoes that are going to last. They are initially more expensive but will prove to be a good purchase. However, a lie is like stealing a pair of flip-flops. The flip-flops weren't very expensive, but the consequences of stealing will cost you a lot. Truth always wins out over a lie. Develop integrity in your life. It will take you farther than you thought you could go.

3. FRIENDS

Have you ever tried to be in the "it" crowd? If it takes a lot of effort to be accepted by people, they probably won't be real friends. We try to buy the right clothes, say the right things, and go to the right places. We let everyone dictate what we believe is right. Have you ever considered not trying to fit in? Just curious. Maybe you could be your own person. That's a novel idea!

Most people want to be accepted and fit in. If this is your only goal, then other people are going to dictate your academic success. I am not proposing that you don't get along with people, but peer pressure can rob you of your life when you try to live for someone's approval. You have to learn to set your own pace, stand your ground, and not be influenced by those around you. Popularity can be short-lived. You have probably experienced that in high school already.

4. VISION

Visualize where you want to be. If watching specific movies or television shows or going certain places is not going to help you succeed, be willing to stand against the peer pressure around you. There is life after college. Remember that when you are in college. You don't want poor decisions posted all over the Internet for years. You are building your life. What kind of life are you building?

One instance specifically comes to mind. I was hanging out with some people at a coffee shop, and they kept talking about all of these movies and TV programs I had never seen. The interesting part was that I didn't care about anything they were talking about. I just sat there. Guess what? We never hung out again. They just weren't helping me get where I needed to go. What kind of people will help you get where you need to go?

5. CONFIDENCE

If you do what everyone else does, you will be in college for four or more years. Determine to be your own person. You will be surprised at the confidence that comes from standing strong on your own two feet.

Confidence is required when going to college. You have to feel comfortable in your own skin and know how to present yourself to other people. Confidence is the ability to be certain of yourself no matter what the circumstances.

How can you become confident? Stop imagining that everyone else has it all together. When you allow your perception of reality to determine your interaction with others, it is hard to be confident. To be confident, you don't have to know it all or have all the answers. But the way you present yourself will make a difference.

The best way to accomplish this is to be confident the first day. The way you start will determine the course of your college experience. Be confident. When you are interacting with others, choose to not be intimidated by your peers. Remember that everyone puts his or her pants on the same way—one leg at a time.

6. HABITS AND VALUES

Developing good habits and values in college is important. One way you can do this is by giving back to your community. When you help other people, you grow in your understanding that the world does not revolve around you. Programs like Big Brothers and Big Sisters are always looking for people to help mentor students in elementary school to high school. The satisfaction and fulfillment you receive from helping others is astounding.

When I was in college, I got involved in a local church, helping with the youth. Being part of a supportive community played a significant role in my life. Many local churches have programs for college students to help connect them with each other and the community.

7. HEALTH AND WELLNESS

When most people think about college, health and exercise are not the first things that come to mind. However, they are important. Exercising regularly and eating healthy will help you stay at your best. The rumored "freshman fifteen" doesn't have to be you. (The freshman fifteen refers to the trend of college students gaining at least fifteen pounds their first year of college.) But if you stress yourself out, never sleep, never exercise, and eat junk food, you are going to be worse off than just fifteen pounds heavier.

I remember my pastor telling a story about developing healthy habits in college. He started exercising every morning at 5:30 a.m. during college. The habit he developed during those years has characterized his life. He committed to something that was beneficial for him for the long haul. If you can't teach an old dog a new trick, teach the young dog a new trick.

How can you be healthy? Exercise at least three times a week. Get involved in an exercise activity on campus, such as racquetball, intramural basketball, or running. Sleep at least eight hours a night. Eat fruits and vegetables. You can't survive on noodles for four years of college and be healthy. It just won't work. However, you can make daily choices about food and exercise that will positively impact your life. Don't underestimate the habits you develop in college. Be intentional in disciplining your life. Build a strong, healthy life.

8. BE THE BEST "YOU"

Who do you admire? It is usually someone who has a quality you want to possess. If you admire a basketball player, implement discipline into your life and see what happens. If you admire a parent, friend, teacher, or pastor, look at their character and commit to becoming that type of person.

Some people live their whole life wishing they could be a certain way. They have an ideal in their mind but think they can never achieve it. No matter what anyone has told you before, you can do anything and be anyone. Even if a parent or teacher has told you that you won't amount to anything, you can rise above their words. Don't let the negative words of your past hold you back. You have the ability to change, to learn, and to grow.

Maybe you have everything going against you. Take heart. There is hope. Obstacles are a part of life. The key is overcoming the obstacles, not just accepting them as fact. Obstacles can be moved. One of my friends had everything going against her. No one in her family had graduated from college. She moved thousands of miles away from home to go to college. Talk about being on your own! She was at a new school in a new city. But her perseverance and determination paved the way for change. She did graduate, and as a result, she is leaving a legacy of "I can," not a history of "I cannot."

Maybe you are in the same boat as my friend. No one in your family has graduated from college. You are up to your eyeballs in obstacles. If so, remember that change happens one day at a time. Make a plan to move forward. Taking just one small step today will help you overcome your obstacles and move in the direction of your goals.

Overcoming obstacles can be directly related to your ability to problem solve. What are your obstacles in going to college? Think of your obstacles as temporary problems that require creative solutions. Don't accept "no" as the final answer in your pursuit of a college degree.

What road are you traveling? We are all on a road, and our decisions dictate our direction. Where are your decisions leading you? Are you setting yourself up to succeed, or are you stuck in a neighborhood where nothing ever changes? You can change your situation. Your life does not have to be dictated by your environment and poor decisions. Don't let the past dictate the present. However, if you don't make a conscious decision to change something, it won't happen on its own. Maybe no one in your family has graduated from college before. Be the first. I am cheering you on.

Here's to you!

ABOUT THE AUTHOR

HONA AMER fast-tracked through college in 2½ years and graduated with her Bachelor of Business Administration degree from Evangel University at age 20. She graduated with her M.B.A. from Missouri State University the same month she turned 22. Today, she enjoys assisting students as they navigate the University experience. She serves as an adjunct college professor and spends as much time as possible writing to help improve the lives of others, including her weekly inspirational message at liveoutlife.com. As the founder of The H Group, Hona also works to assist companies as they utilize 21st century advertising and marketing concepts.

WWW.HONAAMER.COM

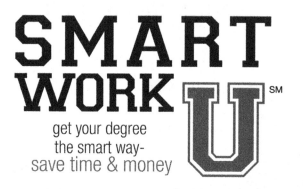

Made in the USA
Monee, IL
04 February 2020

21244698R00085